SOLVING

THE

COMMUNION

ENIGMA

SOLVING THE COMMUNION ENIGMA

what is to come

WHITLEY STRIEBER

foreword by Jeffrey J. Kripal,
chair of Religious Studies, Rice University

JEREMY P. TARCHER/PENGUIN
a member of Penguin Group (USA) Inc.
New York

JEREMY P. TARCHER/PENGUIN
Published by the Penguin Group
Penguin Group (USA) Inc., 375 Hudson Street, New York, New York 10014, USA •
Penguin Group (Canada), 90 Eglinton Avenue East, Suite 700, Toronto, Ontario M4P 2Y3,
Canada (a division of Pearson Penguin Canada Inc.) • Penguin Books Ltd, 80 Strand,
London WC2R 0RL, England • Penguin Ireland, 25 St Stephen's Green, Dublin 2,
Ireland (a division of Penguin Books Ltd) • Penguin Group (Australia), 250 Camberwell Road,
Camberwell, Victoria 3124, Australia (a division of Pearson Australia Group Pty Ltd) •
Penguin Books India Pvt Ltd, 11 Community Centre, Panchsheel Park, New Delhi–110 017,
India • Penguin Group (NZ), 67 Apollo Drive, Rosedale, North Shore 0632, New Zealand
(a division of Pearson New Zealand Ltd) • Penguin Books (South Africa) (Pty) Ltd,
24 Sturdee Avenue, Rosebank, Johannesburg 2196, South Africa

Penguin Books Ltd, Registered Offices: 80 Strand, London WC2R 0RL, England

Most Tarcher/Penguin books are available at special quantity discounts for bulk purchase
for sales promotions, premiums, fund-raising, and educational needs. Special books or book
excerpts also can be created to fit specific needs. For details, write Penguin Group (USA) Inc.
Special Markets, 375 Hudson Street, New York, NY 10014.

Library of Congress Cataloging-in-Publication Data

Strieber, Whitley.
Solving the communion enigma : what is to come / Whitley Strieber ; foreword by Jeffrey J. Kripal.
p.   cm.
Includes bibliographical references.
ISBN 978-1-58542-917-2
1. Unidentified flying objects—Sightings and encounters.   2. Human-alien encounters.   3. Life on
other planets.   I. Title.
TL789.3.S7727   2011   2011046464
001.942—dc23

Printed in the United States of America
1   3   5   7   9   10   8   6   4   2

BOOK DESIGN BY TANYA MAIBORODA

All truth passes through three stages. First, it is ridiculed. Second, it is violently opposed. Third, it is accepted as being self-evident.

—ARTHUR SCHOPENHAUER

*This book is dedicated
to the close-encounter witnesses and those
who have tried to make sense of their dilemma,
on whose shoulders it rests.*

Reading as Mutation

T IS DIFFICULT TO DENY IT ANY LONGER: UFOs are real. This does not mean that we know what they are. We do not. The accent remains squarely on the U, on the Unidentified, on what the folklorist Thomas E. Bullard has recently called the mystery within the myth, the something that yet remains after we have carefully thought our way through the documentation of the sightings, the dubious turns of the conspiracy theorists, and the cultural and media networks of what amounts to a modern mythologization process taking shape right in front of our eyes.[1] The stories themselves are certainly stunning enough: triangular, boomerang, or rectangular ships as big as aircraft carriers (or, in the memorable words of one recent Texan witness, "as big as a Wal-Mart") floating silently over heavily populated areas; green fireballs, flying disks,

_____

1. Thomas E. Bullard, *The Myth and Mystery of UFOs* (Lawrence: University of Kansas, 2010).

and supercraft shutting down nuclear missile silos, floating over nuclear power plants, and effortlessly invading highly sensitive military installations; fighter pilots from Iran to Brazil attempting, always in vain, to engage the things; baffled airline pilots gazing at immense UFOs from the privileged miles-high position of their cockpits; and Chicago O'Hare Airport workers watching a disk float above the United Airlines terminal for five full minutes in broad daylight before it zipped straight up at an impossible speed, punching a perfect hole in the cloud cover.

We are not talking about easily understood misperceptions by lone individuals here. Well-documented UFO waves, like the Hudson Valley sightings of 1983 to 1985 (just a few miles and a few months from where the Strieber story begins), the Belgium wave of 1989 to 1990, or the Phoenix Lights of 1997, were seen *by thousands*, including, in the latter case, by the Republican governor of the state of Arizona, Fife Symington. Nor is it true that we are dealing here with something as vague as fuzzy lights in the sky. People routinely see technological details, specific metallic colors, underbelly structures, tubes, search lights, weird plasmic probes, bubble domes—even, in one famous case involving a security police squadron at an American base in England, markings that looked like Egyptian hieroglyphs on the side of a small triangular craft. Nick Pope, who ran the British Ministry of Defense's UFO unit from 1991 to 1994 and has done as much as anyone to get us on the right track here, had it just right: these are "The Real X-Files."[2]

How any rational person can read this material and not conclude that UFOs are real is beyond me. At this point in the game, dogmatic denial and professional debunking constitute the irrational. Sadly, such

---

2. Leslie Kean, *UFOs: Generals, Pilots, and Government Officials Go on the Record* (New York: Harmony Books, 2010), 162. Kean should be read alongside John B. Alexander, *UFOs: Myths, Conspiracies, and Realities* (New York: St. Martin's Press, 2011). Alexander, a military and intelligence insider, confirms the reality of UFOs but takes a very different stance on what the government really knows: very little.

propaganda and shaming strategies work: not one of the O'Hare witnesses, for example, would speak about the incident in his or her own name, so fearful were they of their jobs. Why *do* we, as a highly educated and supposedly free society, allow these fake rationalisms and this constant censorship campaign to continue unchallenged?

As a historian of religions, I suspect the presence of a taboo here, not in the easy metaphorical or secular sense of that overused word, but in its original sacred sense. So understood, the tabooed is an object or event that violates the proper order and structure of a society and so is anxiously surrounded, walled off, and neutralized—somewhat like an invading disease sets off an immunological response—with rituals and prohibitions of various sorts, often of an extreme and seemingly irrational nature. Such excessive responses mean something here, though, as they eloquently witness to the attempt—always in vain—to preserve the culture's order of knowledge and its illusion of completeness. And such an order, any order (including our present secular scientific order), is *always* incomplete.

The tabooed is not just dangerous, however. It is also sacred—a presence of unimaginable power, potential, and paradox. So too here. As gifted authors like Dr. Jacques Vallée, Bertrand Méheust, and Thomas E. Bullard have shown in great detail, the UFO phenomena is as much about mythical structures and mystical experiences as it is about radar traces and ships in the sky.[3] Until we can deal with this high strangeness as evenly, as honestly, and as subtly as we deal with the government and military reports, we will not, and cannot, understand our situation. We will not take seriously—and I mean *really* seriously—those countless human beings who, as Leslie Kean put it so well, have "been transformed, in one way or another, and sometimes drastically so, by this interaction with the 'impossible.'"[4]

3. For much more on Vallée and Méheust, see my *Authors of the Impossible: The Paranormal and the Sacred* (Chicago: University of Chicago Press, 2010).
4. Kean, *UFOs*, 8.

This is where Whitley Strieber comes in. Whitley is one of our most gifted, prolific, and thoughtful writers on these matters. No doubt, this is partly because he himself is a professional writer, a horror writer and novelist of considerable accomplishments who knows how to structure a sentence and a story. The true source of Strieber's genius, however, lies elsewhere.

Way elsewhere, in an eleven-year ordeal of close encounters with strange beings whom he simply calls "the visitors." He thus understands that the true mystery of the UFO phenomenon, itself a part of a much larger complex of unimaginable things, does not lie with mathematics and machines, but is finally a "deeply and transcendentally human" one. He understands that we sit on an intellectual and spiritual precipice, that a "new world" is just over the horizon, that science and its clunky methods are not going to get us there—in short, that "the greater mystery by far is the human one."

Who has ears to hear such a message?

I am a professional scholar. I analyze and interpret mystical literatures from around the world, "mystical" understood here as a particular kind of "secret" literature that expresses—often through mind-bending paradoxes and the collapse of logical structures—some of the most extreme experiences ever reported of communion, union, even identity with the divine or, if you prefer, with the real. When I first read Whitley's *Communion*, I knew instantly that I was reading a piece of modern mystical literature, something future generations would be reading for decades, if not centuries. The book, after all, possesses all the features that past and present scholars have come to recognize as marks of the mystical:

- extreme alternating responses of fear and attraction, horror and beauty;
- out-of-body flight, often involving a second "subtle" or energetic body;

- paranormal powers, such as precognition, telepathy, and psychokinesis;
- memories, often coded and repressed, of physical or sexual trauma in childhood or youth;
- erotically charged imagery and impossibly intense sexual energies;
- invocations of a secret and subsequent censorship attempts or harassment on the part of established social and/or religious institutions;
- noetic, or "knowing," energies mysteriously transmitted into the body of the visionary;
- life-changing experiences of union or communion with a mysterious alien or Other, who is often paradoxically intuited to be a part of one's own deepest nature; and
- a cognitive "rewiring" and subsequent penchant for thinking beyond all either-or's to something beyond, to a both-and or Third.

Whitley calls the latter impossible thinking "the mystery of the triangle" in *Communion*. We may take it here as the clearest sign of a basic ambiguity or paradox at the very heart of the UFO phenomenon. "Beware," such a Thinker of the Third says in so many words. "Beware of your reasons as much as your beliefs. Do not think in terms of this or that, but in terms of this and that. Certainty is the enemy."

Solving the Communion *Enigma* is a long meditation on this same mystery of the triangle, on this same refusal to think in twos when we should really be thinking in threes. In terms of a genre, the book is a commentary of sorts, a return to *Communion* after a quarter-century: to probe it, query it, criticize it, but perhaps most of all, to draw from it what was only implicit there and make it more explicit here.

Every real writer knows that what he or she puts in a text can never be fully known at the time of the writing, even by the author. We do not just author. We are also authored. We are written as we write, and we are read as we read. Our texts are coded secrets, multidimensional realities that demand multidimensional readings. We might even say that profound texts, like psyches, have their own unconscious. Accordingly, it takes time for the meanings to emerge and be processed in a public, conscious fashion. Only the future can finally read a great book like *Communion*.

Well, we are there, in that future, and here in these pages of *Solving the* Communion *Enigma* we have the privilege to watch a great author return to his most famous text and draw out from it more meaning and more secrets. His conclusions are certainly extraordinary enough: that unanswerable questions can act as an "evolutionary force" that literally rewires the brain; that the secret of the visitor experiences has something to do with the dead and the afterlife; that implants, crop circles, and mutilated animals are all part of the mystery; that the sci-fi motif of "the alien" fails to explain the full spectrum of the encounter experience; that the material world is only the beginning of the human journey; and, perhaps most astonishingly of all, that physical and sexual trauma can "crack open the cosmic egg" and so reveal a "hidden reality" of unimaginable scope. I am not certain that I have ever encountered a mystical writer this fearless, this psychologically astute, and this darn clear.

Early in the book, Whitley recalls his suggestion in *Communion* that the abduction experience "in its totality might be what the force of evolution looks like when it is applied to a conscious mind," which, or so I assume, implies a certain cultural shaping on the part of the imagination. I find this idea endlessly suggestive. I would take it one step further, though, and add that Whitley's books, and especially this book, might well bear a similar function for those of us who have not had the tremendous privilege, and the horrible terror, of an extensive encounter experience. I would suggest that Whitley's books, both fiction and nonfiction alike, are what evolution looks like when it takes up a gifted author, imagination and all, utterly transforms him, and gives him back to us as one of its most nuanced voices and haunting faces.

Be careful what you read in these pages, then. Both the risks and the rewards are very real, for a mind that thinks like this, that writes like this, may well change its ready readers into something else too. Sometimes reading is a kind of mutation.

—JEFFREY J. KRIPAL, chair of Religious Studies, Rice University, and author of *Mutants and Mystics: Science Fiction, Superhero Comics, and the Paranormal*

CONTENTS

PART ONE
The Mystery

T HAS BEEN A QUARTER OF A CENTURY SINCE I PUB-
lished *Communion* and the subsequent two follow-on
books, *Transformation* and *Breakthrough*. These books
described a series of experiences that I had between 1985
and 1994, conventionally known as "close encounters of the third kind"
or "alien abductions."

But are they what they seem?

After the last of these books was published, the experiences continued for a number of years, and left me with discoveries that take
matters far beyond the conventional assumptions. There is an enormous phenomenon unfolding around us that involves UFO sightings,
close encounters, crop circles, and physical effects ranging from the
sublime to the terrifying. It is almost certainly the most complex thing
that has ever happened, but because it is so hard to see in its vastness,
few people realize how much it is actually impacting our lives and our
world.

Individually, each part of the phenomenon is dismissed in a different
way. UFOs are called cases of mistaken identity. And yet, in this book,
I will analyze the sightings reported by one of NASA's most honored
engineers, who was a skilled professional observer of aircraft. "Alien
abductions" are dismissed as folklore, and yet after writing *Communion*, I received hundreds of thousands of detailed accounts, meaning

I

that millions of people have probably had the experience, given how many read the book, and the sensitivity of the subject. It is not folklore. It is part of human life. I will explore what it means. Crop formations are ridiculed as the work of drunks with boards on their feet. And yet some of them are spectacular mysteries.

In fact, every detail of the overall phenomenon is dismissed in some inadequate way, usually with contempt. But why? It's not difficult to argue that it is a genuine mystery and, in fact, the greatest mystery known to man.

Exploring it in as objective a way as I have been able to, I have been led to what I feel are some engaging, if sobering, new speculations about the nature of man and our place in the universe. My discoveries have frightened me deeply, to be frank, but have also disclosed the promise of a glorious unknown that glows at once within us, and beckons us from afar.

I have struggled for twenty years to write this, a true sequel in the sense that it advances the ideas put forth in its predecessors, and doesn't just extend their narrative.

The story I have to tell is so extremely complex and subtle and, above all, so profoundly strange that I have many times despaired of ever being able to write it. Can it be told well and usefully? I can record only what I have seen and what I have come to know about this lurid, bizarre, and wondrous experience, and be as truthful as I am able.

After I published *Communion,* I was immediately—and absurdly, I thought—labeled as an advocate for alien contact. But I have never advocated anything except what I know, which is that there is a genuine question facing us, and one that is important, even urgent, and endlessly tantalizing. Among other things, there is an incredible human element involved that is entirely unremarked in the popular literature, but is certainly one of the great keys to understanding what is, no matter its many outré resonances, also a deeply human experience.

On reading that, some people will conclude that I am repudiating the idea of alien contact. As I have never embraced it, though, I cannot repudiate it, but I certainly don't reject the possibility. The structure of much of the UFO and close-encounter testimony is almost indistinguishable from what a narrative of contact with secretive—and incredibly strange—aliens might be. Or, at least, our idea of what such contact might be.

My original thought after being assaulted in the dead of the night of December 26, 1985, was that I had been the victim of a crime. I had reason to believe, as I will discuss in more detail, that some very unpleasant people might have had a motive to try and drive me mad or, failing that, at least to marginalize me. I recognized one of the individuals who kidnapped me that night. I had known him well, and there was no question about whom I was seeing. He was among aliens, that seemed clear enough, but he was himself no alien, this one. However, when I later attempted to get in touch with him, I began a journey into a deep and transforming human mystery.

At the time, I didn't know what an alien abduction was, and my initial thought was that I was under criminal assault, carried from my home against my will. Only later was I forced to admit to myself that something so unusual had happened to me that it was outside of the scope of criminal law, or any of our codified law, for that matter.

Something about this world of ours simply does not add up. Are secretive aliens here, perhaps working with sinister human forces? Or is something else happening? As I never have before, I think I can now provide some useful focus on these questions.

In *Communion*, I offered the opinion that the experience in its totality might be what the force of evolution looks like when it is applied to a conscious mind. An elegant enough thought, but with it comes the threatening reality of evolutionary change. One has only to consider the dinosaurs to understand the danger of living in an evolutionary moment.

In the third book in the trilogy, *Breakthrough*, I returned to this theme, but now I am able to go further. It is absolutely clear to me that the issue of what the contact experience is remains unresolved, and thus that the question must be preserved. I can describe how the experience is changing us—all of us, not just people who have remembered close encounters. What is happening is happening to the whole world—and is very much facilitated, incidentally, by the fact that it is, for the most part, ignored. Governments are silent and science is unable to face it, so the media denies it and people therefore assume that it's irrelevant. But it is far from that. In fact, not a single human being is unaffected, but almost none of us realize this. It is changing every single one of us on this earth.

If we can get past our refusal to face the reality of the question, the whole nature of our relationship with it can be transformed for the better. There is much to be learned, but we must accept the challenge.

I woke up on the morning of December 27 in a state of disquiet. I remembered violent events. Talking to my old friend about matters that I thought must be classified. Ending up in a strange, messy little room, like a tent. Seeing strange, insectlike figures there. Being raped there.

If I had not been the victim of a crime, then, I thought that I must have a brain tumor or temporal lobe epilepsy, or that I was slipping into psychosis. The physical injuries were what eventually forced me to admit the truth to myself, which was that I had faced the unknown on that night.

Could they be aliens? Something else even more improbable? I became extremely, agonizingly, curious. Night would fall, and I would be tempted to the woods.

I started going out to the location of my original encounter. At first, I was so frightened that I could barely manage to move my legs.

But once I took those first terrified steps toward what I came to call "the visitors," they began to communicate with me. But I must stress that this was, with a few exceptions, not like communicating with other people. I was hardly going out into the woods and sitting down with creatures from another planet. But *something* was happening, and it was no normal or explainable experience.

In truth, the phenomenon, taken as a whole, is so complex and so spectacularly strange that we are best off starting without any assumptions about it at all, beyond the fact that it is real and we do not understand.

What we need to do is determine if any of the physical evidence, and there is a lot of it, can be used to bring the larger question into focus. Much of the structure of what is happening looks very much like contact with an intelligence of some sort that is not human. So, is that what we are facing? If so, what are they?

Being identified as a believer in aliens has always troubled me. It just doesn't seem to me to be the only possible explanation. As profoundly strange as the phenomenon is, for me the most important parts of it have also been deeply human. It is such a lovely mystery, I really cannot see why it is rejected with such opprobrium. But it is, and being an advocate for it makes for a very difficult life.

The reason I hesitate to agree that aliens must be involved is simple: how could they have gotten here? It's easy to say that they came through a "wormhole" or something, or "traveled faster than light," but it is less clear how any sort of the vastly long travel that movement among the stars requires could be accomplished in the real world. Even if some means of propulsion was found that could accelerate a craft of some sort to an appreciable percentage of the speed of light, it would become more and more massive, and thus exponentially harder and harder to control—in the end, impossible to control.

But even if such acceleration was achieved, there is another problem. The universe is so huge that light speed is actually terribly slow. Only a scattering of stars within a hundred light years of earth are even remotely capable of supporting life-bearing planets, and our local region, like all the rest of this vastness we live in, shows not the slightest trace of any sort of residual signal that might suggest that anybody nearby has even passed through a radio age of the sort that we are just now beginning to leave. But our own traces will linger in space, in some sense, for a very long time.

In favor of the alien hypothesis is the fact that small, rocky planets do seem to be quite common. So, almost certainly, "they" are out there. But here? Well, it's really a delicious mystery, because it's possible to view the whole UFO–close-encounter phenomenon as evidence of their presence. But it's equally possible to see it in a very different light. And, in fact, there are elements of it that strongly suggest that the greater mystery by far lies elsewhere.

Nevertheless, I suppose, in a universe this big and this old, it may be that somebody has cut the Gordian knot of interstellar travel. It would surprise me, but I won't reject it out of hand.

In *Communion*, I offered a number of speculations about what they might be. Here, I will explore some of them further and add another: we may have structural limitations in our brains that prevent us from articulating what they are, in the same sense that a chimpanzee can never accurately understand, say, a car. Indeed, this may be the reason that they are presenting us with the challenge that we face: unanswerable questions literally change the brain.

Could they be using their own mysterious presence to alter our brains in such a way that we *can* understand? If they are a "force of evolution," perhaps this is their intention.

Whatever they are, our visitors are very secretive, so secrecy must be useful to them. There are a number of reasons why they might conceal themselves—among them, obviously, the fact that we would not like what they are or what they are doing, if we understood. But as long as we continue to ignore them, one thing is clear: they are in control.

It wouldn't be that difficult to change this, at least somewhat. If we apply our existing scientific skills to the physical evidence that they have already left behind, we can take the measure of both any threat they represent and the promise that they offer.

If we face them, one way or another, we are going to find ourselves living in what amounts to a new world.

Can we bear it? Dare we?

There is only one way to find out: indulge this most tantalizing of questions.

CHAPTER 1
Turning the Secret Key

I
N MY LIFE, I WENT IN A MATTER OF MONTHS FROM indifference to the idea of UFOs and visitors to the shock of close encounter and the realization that I was confronting something real. My initial thought was that I had been criminally assaulted, and, as I have learned more about what happened to me on the night of my close encounter, that has remained a possibility. I may have been assaulted both by people who are—or should be—subject to ordinary human law and by something very much stranger, and far outside of our laws.

As I have said, it is not at all clear that the final resolution of the mystery will involve creatures from another planet. Among other things, since I wrote *Communion*, science has determined that parallel universes may be physically real and that time travel may in some way be possible. At the same time, though, it is becoming clear that we don't actually understand movement all that well, not when things like quantum entanglement can be physically demonstrated to result in instantaneous communication over unlimited distance, and large-sized objects, not just tiny ones, can be made to exist in two states at the same time.

Right now the question that science generally asks is the same one that has been asked for sixty years: are flying saucers real or not? And since interstellar travel would appear to be impossible, the answer must be no. Or so the reasoning goes.

Many skilled observers have seen unidentified flying objects. I will discuss the observations of just one of them, Dr. Paul Hill of NASA. With his credentials, his analysis of what he had seen should have been treated with the utmost seriousness. Instead, NASA suppressed his book, *Unconventional Flying Objects*, which was published only after his death.

But that's just the matter of the unidentified flying objects. There is much more. There is the question of objects that have been implanted into people, a claim hastily dismissed but actually compelling and disturbing. There has been some surprising scientific work done on such objects, and they are far from easy to explain. There is one case in particular that has some extremely strange features: it is my own. I received an implant in May of 1989, but not from aliens. I was wide awake when it happened, and people were responsible. I saw them perfectly clearly. If I met them again, I could identify them easily. I will discuss these events in detail in a later chapter, as well as describe the attempt to surgically remove the object, and what was discovered about it. The thing is a credibly verified mystery—that I carry to this day in my left ear.

Speaking of credibility, there are credible professional witnesses to UFOs, and implants are much more difficult to explain away than most of us have been led to believe. There is also a great deal more evidence that the whole bizarre phenomenon, from UFOs to abductions to crop formations—all of it—is in some way physically real, and some of that evidence is wondrous and some of it is shocking, but all of it is far more compelling—and far stranger—than one would expect.

But what of the dialogue about all this? In the sixty years since it first began, it has gone absolutely nowhere.

The fact that the debate is still in the same place today that it was in 1950 is, in part, due to an emotional unwillingness to entertain the notion that somebody with greater powers may be here who won't deal openly with us. We need to get past resistance of that sort, and confront the much more important issues of just which of our social institutions are appropriately equipped to deal with these phenomena, and how we go about exploring the physical evidence that is already available.

The event that unfolded in my life on December 26, 1985, was frightening and assaultive, but also filled with wonder. Over the next few months, as I forced myself to swallow my terror and turn toward my assailants, they reacted with the richest, most complex, and most profoundly improbable response that I think it is possible to imagine.

While I have been marginalized and generally dismissed as an advocate of belief in aliens, I have also benefited immeasurably from my experience. But also, I have seen things and learned things that are disturbing, and I haven't the slightest intention of ignoring them. If we are going to face our visitors, we have to face all they have on offer, from the grace to the horror and all that lies between.

My understanding of life, being, and the world was completely overturned and revised by what happened to me. I say "my," but my wife Anne and I endured this together. She encountered the visitors in a physical sense only once, and then just very briefly, but she brought rigor and dimension to the narrative we have developed about our experience, which would never have been there without her carefully skeptical mind. She also read the vast outpouring of correspondence we received from other people who had similar experiences, and digested this knowledge for us both.

She sat at her desk by the hour, by the day, for years, reading and categorizing letters, and storing many of them in her prodigious memory.

She also made what I believe is the single most important discovery of all when she wrote on her chalkboard: "This has something to do with death."

It does have something to do with death. In fact, it has to do with the next stage in the evolution of this species, which involves a leap ahead into a completely new relationship with ourselves, in which mysteries like death take on an entirely new meaning.

But what is that meaning? Where are we going as a species? What is the fate of man?

Hardly questions to ask, say, a metallurgist. But it might be useful to ask him about whether or not an implant is really an unexplained foreign body, or something generated by biological processes.

If he concludes that it's an unexplained foreign body, though, we're going to be at the edge of a phenomenological cliff, and I doubt that, when we take the leap, scientific method as we understand it now is going to be all that useful a tool in coming to terms with what we find.

This is why I have titled this book *Solving the* Communion *Enigma*. Because, truly, we have unfolding before us an incredible possibility, a journey into a new way of being that is as far from where we are now as the human mind is from that of the animals.

Anne saw from the beginning that keeping the question open was essential to change of mind, and we learned together how to do that. The more nuanced our questions, the more richly dimensional our visitors' responses became.

If you go on the Internet, you'll be told that the visitors are aliens. Many different stars will be identified as their points of origin. Many different species will be described in detail. Prominent among them will be "the grays," who were first portrayed, as far as I have been able to discover, on the cover of the June 1957 *Fantastic Universe* science-fiction magazine, and who became an iconic alien image with the publication of *Communion*.

From the morning of December 27, when I woke up in pain and

reeling with confusion, I have wondered: *Why me?* It's a question I've been asked a thousand times, and asked myself again and again. And I have been asked it, also, by others who are also in contact, and have nowhere to turn and no way to make it stop: *Why me, why us?*

People assume that close encounters are reserved to just a few of us, but it seems equally likely to me that what is really happening is that just a few of us remember what is actually a very common part of the human experience.

But why does one remember and not another?

There is an answer. It comes out of the darkest depths of human experience, and out of childhood.

CHAPTER 2

The Mirror Shattered

E VERYONE WHO HAS EVER WONDERED ABOUT
UFOs or alien contact, speculated about crop
formations, or been disturbed by weird animal
mutilations, has been changed by the question
raised by these enigmas. And the more intensely the question has been
felt, the more profound the change that has taken place.

But there is a certain smaller group who has gone beyond the
question. The lives of these people have been completely upended
by the unimaginable power of the phenomenon. These are the close-
encounter witnesses. For the most part, the witnesses report encounters with what appear to be aliens. I am one of the few who has seen
people and aliens together. During my 1985 encounter, I saw an old
friend whom, as he had told me some years before, had recently retired
from the CIA. He was with these seeming aliens. Afterward, I found
out from a relative of his that in December of 1985 when I saw him
and talked to him, he had been dead for months.

It's one thing to wonder about UFOs but another matter entirely to find oneself confronting their occupants, and more incredibly, human helpers who are not even alive.

For most of the past twenty-five years, I have not been able to offer a clear answer to the question of why one person will become entangled in direct contact and another won't. At the same time, I have come to think that contact is not rare. As some of the most remarkable cases suggest, it may be, effectively, universal. What is rare is noticing it.

A study published by Dr. Kenneth Ring in his book *The Omega Project* offered the germ of an answer to the question of why this would be so. One thing that stood out in this study of near-death experiencers and close-encounter witnesses was that they remembered childhood trauma of various kinds—not necessarily sexual trauma, but trauma. Ring reported "a most intriguing, clear-cut and disturbing pattern. There is a consistent tendency for both UFO and near-death experiencers to report a greater incidence of child-abuse and trauma." They appeared at "highly significant statistical levels."

When I first read this, I looked back over my own childhood and couldn't remember any particular trauma except a series of family tragedies that happened when I was eleven and twelve. By contrast, Anne had a very traumatic memory. When she was seven, she'd found her mother dead. She had committed suicide.

For her, the mirror of expectation was shattered. She was therefore an ideal candidate to see things that people with intact expectations routinely filter out.

But she wasn't the one having the bizarre experiences—I was. Or so it seemed at the time. A closer look tells a different story, but more about that later.

In 1994, we moved to Texas, and I began revisiting the haunts of my childhood, because I did have rather vivid memories of child-hood close encounters. Amazingly, I found the place where they had unfolded, on the edge of a flood zone near my old neighborhood in

San Antonio called Olmos Basin. I didn't just find a general area but the specific spot—a group of ruined benches—which I had described in detail prior to locating them.

I wrote a book about these experiences called *The Secret School*. Although I turned up witnesses who also remembered enough to suggest that there had been something real happening, and something very unusual, I cannot to this day be certain about what it was, as I made clear in the book.

None of it seemed particularly traumatic. It was rather magical, actually. I don't recall much fear. So perhaps my personal expectations about reality hadn't been shattered in childhood. Perhaps there was another reason that I had been drawn into close encounter.

Or was there? There are other memories that I found myself looking at anew after an odd incident one afternoon in December of 1999. These memories had always been in my mind, but I hadn't known exactly what they were about, and so had left them unexamined.

After this event, though, that began to change. I began to wonder about the memories. I began to research them.

And I found, hidden in my own past, a shattered childhood.

In the autumn of 1999, Anne and I went with my brother to a pet show northeast of San Antonio, in the town of Universal City.

We were driving back on Interstate 35, a large and well-trafficked highway, when I suddenly found myself on a two-lane road amid rolling fields.

I was shocked. I had been on a busy interstate. Now I was out in the country. Anne was still sitting quietly beside me. I had no idea where we were.

We came to a gate made of chain-link fencing, and the coldest, eeriest feeling spread through me. It was the south gate to Randolph Air Force Base, and I remembered it from before—from another, distant time, another life.

Anne said, "Where are we? Why have we stopped?"

I didn't know how to answer her. I must have taken an exit off 35 and ended up here. But why did I have no memory of doing it?

I said, "I remember this place. South Gate." I stared at the closed chain-link gate. Beyond it, I could see some old buildings. "This is Randolph," I added. "Randolph Air Force Base."

An old memory came into focus: I was sitting in the front seat of a car, and small enough that I was looking at the glove box, not out the windshield. I knew, though, that we were entering South Gate.

I said to Anne, "I came here when I was a child." But why? With whom?

Anne, who has a great deal of knowledge about the pitfalls of memory, knew to say nothing.

My stomach suddenly became acidic. I could hardly breathe. I had become so tense that I could hardly pull my hands off the steering wheel.

When I was a child, we'd sometimes come to Randolph for air shows, but I recalled entering by the front gate. I couldn't understand why we might have come this way, or why it frightened me so much.

I said to her, "Did you notice anything unusual about my driving just now?"

She said, "No, nothing."

She is not comfortable in cars. She doesn't like highways. Anything strange would have caused an immediate reaction on her part.

"Did you notice us taking an exit?"

"Yes, but everything seemed normal."

"Did I say anything?"

"No. I thought we were about home."

It was a logical assumption. She wasn't familiar with the area, and didn't know one exit from another.

So I was mystified by my own behavior. How could I possibly have taken an exit so obviously wrong on a highway I'd been traveling since I learned to drive? But I hadn't just taken an exit and ended up here. To do this, I had to find the Lower Seguin Road, then this disused gate, then turn and face the car toward the gate, all without realizing what I was doing.

But I had done this, without question. We were here. I was staring right at the gate.

Finally, I did the only thing I could do—I turned around and drove home. On that afternoon, I left Randolph behind, but something from my deepest past came with me.

I was what could charitably be called an "active" little boy. When I was four, I had been placed in the kindergarten run by the Sisters of the Incarnate Word, in a tiny red-brick building on the campus of what is now Incarnate Word University.

My time there ended abruptly when I thrust a friction toy under a sister's habit. Her underthings became tangled in the whirring mechanism. To put it mildly, she was agitated.

It was decided that I was too rambunctious for the sisters, and I was sent instead to Jack Tolar's River Ranch Day Camp on Austin Highway.

Now, as we passed the ruins of the old day camp on our way home to Alamo Heights, a strange sort of feeling went through me. I had loved the camp. So what was this faint sense of disquiet?

Certain memories from my very early childhood, strange memories that I had always more or less ignored, now seemed to need to be addressed a little more carefully. This is because they might have involved both the day camp and Randolph. They were disturbing, as they always had been.

Most of my memories of the day camp are fond ones. I learned to swim there, and had quite a few adventures. I was bucked off a horse during a camp parade, dramatic fun for a child like me. My best friend got his penis caught in a bicycle pump, and the fire department had to be called to free him. More excitement, seeing the big fire trucks. Never mind that his mother was having hysterics as they used their hacksaw. On a nature hike, I was playing with a stick and managed to knock down a hornet's nest, which hit Jack Tolar in the back of the head. Like the discomfited nun, he was, to say the least, agitated. But he could handle little boys very well, and there was no question about my being expelled. He described what would happen to me if I ever did anything like that again but—very cleverly—withheld the details. Never again did I pull anything like that at Jack Tolar's.

While my memories of the day camp are full of joy and excitement and fun, there was a counselor there who may have done some things she should not have—never on camp property, and, I feel sure, without the Tolar family's knowledge. Jack Tolar taught me to swim, and, thirty-five years later, taught my son to swim. In all that time, there was not the slightest indication of there being anything wrong about him or any of the programs he ran.

But nobody can supervise his employees all the time, and I recall some very peculiar incidents involving this counselor.

Once, she drove me and a number of other children to a place with a big gate and lots of trees, where we were taken into a large house and given teddy bears to play with while being told how wonderful Stalin was.

In 1949 when this event took place, there were still many Americans who revered Stalin and the USSR. The Russian people had just bled themselves white in pursuit of victory in World War II. But anti-communism was becoming an important social force, about to displace the misguided faith of Franklin Roosevelt in his friend "Uncle Joe" Stalin, who was coming to be seen for what he was: a monster. Yet, many on the far left clung to their reverence for him.

Still, why in the world anybody would think to propagandize a gaggle of tiny children about Stalin, I cannot imagine. Certainly, it didn't sink in. In 1953 I sat by the radio, listening to the bulletin that Stalin had died, and felt a terrific sense of relief.

But that is only one strange memory from those early days that involves her. The others are much darker.

I have hinted at them in other narratives of my childhood. In the transcript of my session with Dr. Donald Klein that is reproduced in *Communion*, for example, there is brief mention of a fear of telephone booths.

This is why: I recall getting into what I thought was an elevator in a place where there were men in uniform, a place I believe to have been Randolph. But it became dead dark and I began to feel people touching me. They were very close. Crammed in. I recall heat and terrific fear and a great deal of noise.

The memory is not of an elevator. Apparently I was told it was an elevator before I would go in. It was actually a much more confined space, and I was trapped in it, crammed in with other children.

I also remember seeing a tall black cabinet, like a phone booth painted black, which was the origin of my fear of phone booths, and was probably the place where we had been put. Why this was done, I do not remember, or, more probably, it was never explained.

There was a man who came to my childhood home called Dr. Krauss or Dr. Krause. He spoke with a strange mixture of a German and a Spanish accent. Often, he wore a uniform. When he appeared, I can recall feeling great fear.

To escape him, I once climbed out of the window of my sister's bedroom and onto the roof of the wing where my parents lived. Then I went up onto the second-story roof and literally begged to be taken away into the sky. But he climbed up after me and took me instead.

This would have been after my eighth or ninth birthday, because my parents' wing wasn't built until I was seven, and I was not able to climb up from one roof to the next until my eighth summer.

The first time I met Dr. Krause was in what I assume must have been the counselor's house, when I was five. She took me there one day after camp. When we went into her living room there was a man there wearing a white Mexican guayabera. My counselor went off into the back of the house, leaving me with him. When he wouldn't speak, I became uneasy and ran after her.

I was appalled to find her lying on her side on a bed with her hands behind her back and an expression of horror on her face. She appeared to be tied up. I tried to leave the house, but the man blocked my way.

That's my last recollection of that particular moment, but even now I can feel the fear that overcame me as I faced, as a tiny child, a situation that was terribly wrong and a person who was horrifying to me.

I assume that the blackness that follows my last image of the man, as he stood blocking my way to the front door, conceals my capture by him, and what else was then done to me.

This is the first of a long series of memories, always just the briefest snatches, always distressing and confusing. Who were these people? What were they doing to me?

I have written very little about them before, because I have not been able to find any trace of any of the people involved. The day camp is long gone, and as far as I have been able to determine, there are no records left from its operations in the late forties.

One counselor was Laverne McMillan, but I remember her well and she was not the person whose face is in my memory. She was a childhood friend of my sixth-grade teacher, and the daughter of San Antonio residents Mr. and Mrs. L. J. McMillan.

I remember Laverne clearly because she was on the school's station wagon when it was hit by a bus at the end of our street in July of 1951. Nobody was killed, but the accident was so loud that we heard it. I was not going to camp that day because I was nauseated, which would happen more and more often over the next few months.

My mother and I jumped in her car immediately and drove up the street. And there was the camp station wagon with a city bus practically on top of it. Mrs. Tolar was standing beside it with her skirt covered with blood, and Laverne had gotten all the children onto the side of the street.

The police came, followed by what appeared to me to be every ambulance in San Antonio and a cavalcade of parents. Mrs. Tolar and some of the children went off in the ambulances, and the other kids were taken home.

Had I not felt so ill, I would have been in the station wagon when it was hit, so I was to some degree lucky that morning.

It does seem as if I was living under some sort of pressure even then, but in the bosom of a very quiet southern family. By the summer of 1951, I had been going to Jack Tolar's for three years, and was getting ready to start second grade at Mount Sacred Heart School.

Our lives proceeded with a measured formality. Summers meant camp in the mornings and afternoons at the San Antonio Country Club, swimming and playing sports. During school days, breakfast was at seven, then I was off to school in my neat uniform, my shoes and brass carefully polished. At three-fifteen Mother would pick me up and take me home. I would do my homework, then straighten up and go down to dinner at six, still in my uniform. My father would be in coat and tie, my mother and sister neatly dressed. There would be the blessing, then our maid, Annie, would serve us.

Annie and my parents were protective and loving toward us children. It was a settled family where voices were rarely raised. Of course there were tensions, but we children were hardly aware of them.

But under the surface there was, at least for me, a creeping terror present in my life. Perhaps my memories involve a pederast who had originally been facilitated by a young camp counselor, and whose actions had no official standing and no connection to Randolph.

Or did they?

I am far from being the only person with memories of horrendous childhood experiences on military facilities. And, in fact, I think that it's possible that something terrible was done to children in those days, and that it might even have continued long after, perhaps even to this day.

Whether that is true or not, one thing is clear: the pressure was very real, so real that in October of my seventh year, I became so beset with sickness after sickness that blood tests were carried out, and it was discovered that I had lost my immunity to disease. My white-blood-cell count was dangerously and abnormally low.

Infections of various kinds, congenital disorders, and exhaustion can all lead to a depressed white-blood-cell count, but I don't have any congenital disorders that would have caused this. However, I was certainly exhausted. I suffered from nightmares and daytime dread and was in a state of extreme stress.

I was treated at the U.S. Army's Brooke General Hospital with gamma-globulin injections. Dr. Krause's visits also stopped, at least for a while, and by the next January I was well enough to return to school.

But what had happened? I brought this up with my parents a number of times, but they were unclear about it. My father couldn't speak of it without becoming upset. It made him pace. I assumed that this was because he had nearly lost his child. He would say only that something had gone wrong.

Dr. Krause returned to my life that spring, but his visits were just occasional. Nevertheless, in the summer of my ninth year, I became extremely ill again. I was once again isolated. It had been fine with me to be unable to go to school when I was seven. But, as I reported in *The Secret School*, I was not so pleased to have to stay inside during summer vacation.

I remember a tremendous sense of pressure and tension continuing through those years. Something was overwhelming me. Many of the nightmares involved seeing filthy children in cages and being threatened with the same treatment if I told my parents anything. I recall being told that my mother and father would go to jail if I revealed what Dr. Krause and I were doing together. I was terrified for their welfare.

When Dr. Krause came, it was like a demon emerging from hell. If

I refused to go with him, I was frightened that my parents would be hurt, so I put a smile on my face and I went, and every time I went, I recall deafening noise and confinement in blackness and devastating dread.

I recall other things too—a frightening trip with him to Mexico, I believe to Monterrey. I was told that I was being taken to a special school. I recall driving up into the hills above Monterrey, to a large white house on a steep street.

I saw things there that were unspeakable. There was blood, and there were children I was told were from Israel, and they were in terrible shape. I remember that they were very dirty, and they had been beaten. I recall no other details, but what I do remember has haunted me all of my life.

I was very young when these things happened. Whatever they were, they certainly shattered the mirror of expectation for me, leaving me, like my wife and so many other people whose understanding of reality has been upended in childhood, open from then on to noticing what most people assume to be impossible and therefore do not see.

Once the mirror of expectation is shattered, the door of perception is open, and there is something there, something alive, looking back at us from where the mirror once stood.

These memories have been with me for a long time. They aren't recovered memories, or memories that surfaced after many years, or "flashbulb memories." They are natural memories, undisturbed but not understood, carefully compartmentalized and ignored.

I always hesitated to write about them because of the explosive implications that children were being abused under some very distasteful circumstances by people with some sort of official brief.

I wouldn't record them now but for a distinct whiff of corroboration.

While I cannot prove that any of this actually involved trips to Randolph and horrible classes held there, that is what I remember. But the mind of a child is not necessarily going to be a repository of accurate memories, especially when high levels of fear and tension are involved.

However, there is a bottom line here, and it is that whatever was really happening, the pressure was severe enough to threaten my health.

My mother was not a saver of memorabilia. There are only a few photographs left from my childhood, but there is one thing that she kept, and that is my second-grade report card that includes the record of my long absence from school from October of 1951 until January of 1952. When I look at it, I think of how reticent she and my father were to talk about what had gone wrong, beyond saying that they didn't know why it had happened.

I asked my mother about Dr. Krause. She told me that she did not remember him. I asked my father about the trip to Monterrey. He said that we had taken it together, and stayed in the Ancira Hotel while we were there. I remember flying down in a very noisy airplane. When I asked my father why we had gone and who had gone with us, he simply shook his head and said, "It was a business trip."

Many years later, I went back to the Ancira to see if it seemed familiar to me. One thing did: an elaborate buffet. I remembered it clearly.

My father had some secrets. When I was about twelve, he gave me a desk from his office to use in my room, and after the workmen had set it up and left, I found a photograph stuck in a crack in the top of one of the drawers. It was of my father. It had been taken in what looked like a North African setting. There was a coffin being held up by two men in soutanes and fezzes. Lying in the coffin with his eyes closed and his hands folded on his chest was my father.

Of course I was amazed by this picture and took it to him immediately to ask what it was. He ripped it into small pieces and flushed it down the toilet. He never said a single word about it.

Some time between the ages of seven and nine, the visits from Dr. Krause stopped altogether. My parents had had loud arguments with him. He'd left the house angry. There had been phone calls. One after-noon, a small plane came and began diving at the house, coming low. I was excited and called my father to come and see.

He was horrified and hustled me into the house. I can very well remember how my excitement changed to fear, because he was afraid.

These memories prove nothing and explain nothing. The only proof of anything is the immune-system failure, but I was also frightened of my second-grade teacher, so perhaps that explains it.

And yet, I cannot help but feel that I am being too conservative with these memories. I don't want them to be what they seem, which are the memories of a child who was being subjected to abuse that did have some sort of official context, and should never, ever have been allowed.

Over the past ten years, I've done research into the question of whether or not there might have been a program that placed children under pressure in order to do something like induce split personalities, or for whatever demented reason.

The most famous case I discovered was that of Candy Jones, who claimed that CIA mind-control experts had created a second personality in her using hypnosis, and that this second personality carried out assignments that the first personality did not remember.

In 2004, I interviewed Donald Bain, the author of *The Control of Candy Jones*, for my radio program, *Dreamland*. By then I had accumulated some evidence that such programs might have existed, and I was hoping that Bain would provide concrete proof.

That did not happen, and I have no idea whether or not Candy Jones's story is true. But hers is not the only such claim, and there are other, more concrete, reports that suggest that something dreadful has been done, and is still being concealed.

While I don't feel that I have a split personality, I have to wonder. For example, how did I end up driving to that old gate? Who was driving the car? Not the person writing this narrative. Somewhere along

I-35, I disappeared and another person took over the driving chore, a person who apparently remembers that gate very well, and is, I suspect, striving to tell a story that he is supposed to have suppressed forever, a story that I am telling now, on behalf of the brutalized child who still suffers within me.

Despite as extensive a search as I have been able to mount, I have never found anyone with a name even close to Antonio Krause who could have been involved with me in the way that I remember. Somebody was, though. That may not have been his name, but I am reasonably sure that the man was real.

There were at Randolph in those days a number of former Nazi scientists working under Dr. Hubertus Strughold at the School of Aviation Medicine. Dr. Strughold and the others had been brought here through Project Paperclip, which was designed to make use of Nazi scientists who could help develop American military programs.

Dr. Strughold was much honored in his early days at Randolph, but it later became known that during the war, he had been aware of experiments at Dachau in which people were, among other things, slowly murdered in vats of ice water in order to devise ways of saving the lives of German pilots who crashed into frigid waters. Others were killed in pressure chambers by either being hyperoxegnated or having the air slowly removed, so that the effects of both anoxia and hyperoxia could be observed.

The victims were placed in a cabinet that had been built by the Luftwaffe, a primitive pressure chamber. Their sufferings could be watched through a small window, and Dr. Strughold may well have been one of the observers. At Randolph, he worked extensively on questions of how the human body reacts to extremely low air pressure and lack of oxygen.

I wasn't subjected to experiments involving air pressure, but I surely do remember some sort of very confined space like that cabinet.

There were also mind-control experiments at Dachau involving hypnosis and the use of high doses of mescaline. The U.S. Navy's Project Chatter, begun shortly after the war and employing some of the scientists who had engaged in these experiments, was intended to develop means of getting people to become highly responsive to interrogation using drugs and hypnotic techniques, and drugs such as Metroniazole were used in interrogations from 1946 on.

But were children involved? In the camps, they were notoriously used as experimental subjects. But would any civilized military authority go so far as to put children in such jeopardy? And what sort of parents would tolerate it?

Perhaps parents who had been misled, as I believe mine were. Otherwise, why would I have been threatened in the way I was? Why would I have had to do my best to act as if nothing was wrong?

I think that my parents eventually understood that whatever I was being made to endure was causing me harm, and got me out of the program.

I have a very close friend in San Antonio whose father once defended a man who was charged with treason during the Korean War. He won the case, and the U.S. military was seriously embarrassed.

My friend, now a distinguished academic, remembers that his parents were visited by an Air Force couple not long after the trial, who told them that there was a special program at Randolph for gifted children, and that their son might benefit from it. They were Skinnerians and claimed that they were raising their own child in a Skinner box. My friend's parents were not comfortable with this couple and, fortunately for him, declined to pursue the matter. He remembers the incident well, though, as he was in the room during the visit.

Perhaps my parents were not as discerning as his.

However, it is also true that I have a wide acquaintance in San Antonio, and only this one man has had any knowledge of any unusual children's group at Randolph.

Nevertheless, something happened to put me under tremendous

pressure in those days, and I think that the shattering of my expectations about reality that resulted has colored the rest of my life, just as my wife's discovery of her dead mother forever shattered her expectations.

Even so, I probably would not have written about any of these matters had I not discovered two other cases, one involving testimony before President Clinton's Advisory Committee on Human Radiation Experiments, and the other the curious and disturbing story of the Finders.

CHAPTER 3
The Lost Finders

IN THE *U.S. NEWS & WORLD REPORT* ISSUE OF December 27, 1993, there appears a very strange story about a group called the Finders. The story was first reported in *The Washington Post* on February 7, 1987, and involved the discovery, in a Tallahassee park, of six "disheveled" children who were being supervised by two well-dressed men. Concerned residents called the police, who found the children in a dirty and unkempt condition. They ranged in age from four to six, and only one of them would talk.

The men explained that they were part of an organization called the Finders, a Washington group who sought out brilliant children in order to help them get educated to their full potential.

This seems innocuous enough, but the children involved were filthy and hungry, and apparently did not know their own names. As it appeared that international child trafficking might be involved, customs agents investigated the case.

Their report of February 12, 1987, states, "This office was contacted by the Tallahassee Police Department on February 5, 1987, who requested assistance in attempting to identify two adult males and six minor children, all taken into custody the previous day. The men, arrested and charged with multiple counts of child abuse, were being very evasive with police in the questions being asked of them pursuant the children and their condition."

The report continues, "The police had received an anonymous telephone call relative to two well-dressed white men wearing suits and ties in Myers Park (Tallahassee), apparently watching six dirty and unkempt children in the playground area. HOULIHAN and AMMERMAN were near a 1980 blue Dodge van bearing Virginia license number XHW-557, the inside of which was later described as foul-smelling, filled with maps, books, letters, and with a mattress situated to the rear of the van which appeared as if it were used as a bed, and the overall appearance of the van gave the impression that all eight persons were living in it.

"The children were covered with insect bites, were very dirty, most of the children were not wearing underwear and all of the children had not been bathed in many days.

"The men were arrested and charged with multiple counts of child abuse and lodged in the Leon County Jail. Once in custody the men were somewhat evasive in their answers to the police regarding the children and stated only that they both were the children's teachers and that all were enroute to Mexico to establish a school for brilliant children."

Something in that document almost stopped my heart: the two men reported as supervising the children, Douglas Ammerman and Michael Houlihan, had explained that they were "transporting these children to Mexico and a school for brilliant children."

Was it the same place that I had been taken in Monterrey? Did it still exist in 1985? Does it now?

I came across the Finders story in 1995, which decided me to make my visit to Monterrey. When I returned in 1996, I recognized details of the Ancira easily enough. We stayed there and even ate at the famous buffet, which was still spectacular.

I drove up and down in the hills above the city, trying to find the mansion where I had been taken. But I could not find the house. Nothing struck a familiar chord. If only I'd had a street name or an address, I could have organized a records search, but I was unsuccessful.

I had a vague memory that the house had been connected to the Pan American Sulfur Company, which had been formed in 1947 to exploit sulfur deposits in Mexico. But I could find no evidence that any of the principals, who were from Dallas, had ever lived in Monterrey.

The trail of the children found in Tallahassee led back to Washington, D.C., and the Finders group, whose leader, Marion Pettie, claimed that nothing illegal was being done.

Citing the National Security Act, the CIA took over the investigation, stating that it was an "internal matter."

Although the Justice Department announced at the time that a "continuing investigation" was in progress, nothing was ever released suggesting that the Finders were more than a rather eccentric group, and nothing was ever revealed about any school in Mexico.

Florida representative Tom Lewis is quoted by *U.S. News* as saying, "Could our own government have something to do with this Finders organization and turned their backs on these children? That's what all the evidence points to."

There is another reference in the report that haunts me, to files discovered in the Finders' headquarters, which included a "Palestinian" file.

When I read that, I wondered about the children I had seen. Why did I know that they were Jewish? Above all, why were they in such awful shape?

The Finders case has apparently been classified. The members of the organization have maintained that nothing illegal was going on.

But it certainly does not appear that the children discovered in the Tallahassee park were well treated, and it does seem inappropriate that the investigation was quashed.

My conclusion is that the whole matter of possible child experimentation and child abuse at an official level calls for more investigation, and I think that the victims, if there are any, are owed an apology such as that given to the adult victims of the notorious plutonium experiments by President Clinton, on behalf of the U.S. government.

It seems that people were exposed without their knowledge to high levels of radiation during the 1950s. Their story was brilliantly told by Pulitzer Prize winner Eileen Welsome in her *The Plutonium Files*, which led to the exposure of bizarre crimes that involved tricking innocent people into sleeping in radioactive rooms or eating radioactive food, all in the name of determining how radiation poisoning works.

The book makes for harrowing reading, and it shows quite clearly that officials were perfectly willing to engage in the most atrocious abuse of adult American citizens. In pursuit of more information, I also interviewed Eileen Welsome, but she told me that she had not come across any indication that children were involved in any of the experiments she had uncovered, and she wasn't aware of any other information about the subject.

There was also the CIA's notorious MK-ULTRA mind-control project that became a media sensation when it was revealed by a congressional committee in 1975. The committee's attention had been attracted by a report in *The New York Times* in 1974 revealing the fact that the CIA had engaged in illegal domestic activities in the 1960s, which included experimentation on U.S. citizens.

Even though CIA director Richard Helms had ordered MK-ULTRA's files destroyed in 1973, the Senate Select Committee to Study Governmental Operations with Respect to Intelligence Activities, chaired by Senator Frank Church, was able to determine that the

CIA's Office of Scientific Intelligence had, from the early 1950s and into the late 1960s, conducted mind-control and interrogation experiments on unwitting subjects that involved the use of drugs such as LSD, sensory deprivation, and attempts to split personalities in order to create agents who had hidden personalities that could be secretly made to follow orders, but who would be consciously unaware of their own activities. Despite Helms's efforts, twenty thousand documents were uncovered using the Freedom of Information Act. (Helms had destroyed the files in 1973, just before the act came into force.) Among the documents are only four that make reference to programs involving children, and these appear to be benign—a study of the social dynamics of gangs, an attempt to find possible future agents among foreign children in the U.S., and a couple of other reasonably straightforward programs.

However, two boxes of the files that were found remained sealed despite a court battle. The judge ruled that they were still too sensitive to be subject to Freedom of Information release.

I have often wondered if they detail experiments on children.

After the publication of *The Plutonium Files*, which documents the fantastically evil abuse of American citizens by the Atomic Energy Commission, President Clinton convened his Advisory Committee on Human Radiation Experiments to look more deeply into the documentation that had been discovered.

A social worker, Valerie B. Wolf of New Orleans, testified before the committee, along with one of her clients, Claudia S. Mullen, to the effect that Ms. Mullen had been subjected, as a child, to the same sort of abuse that I remember. I wondered, then, if others remember the same thing, how could it be that it didn't happen? My memories date from long before I heard anything about Claudia Mullen or Candy Jones or anyone else who experienced such things.

Valerie Wolf testified that many of the victims of this sort of abuse suffered from muscle and connective tissue disorder "as well as mysterious ailments for which a diagnosis cannot be found." And for that matter, why was a seven-year-old boy being treated at a military hospital at all? My father wasn't in the military. Why wasn't I treated at a local hospital, or by my own doctor? He was a distinguished local pediatrician of impeccable reputation called Sidney Kaliski, and certainly would have been capable of treating me.

Valerie Wolf's client and her sisters suffer from ailments suggestive of radiation poisoning, but I have to say that since childhood, I have had only one major illness, which was appendicitis that was misdiagnosed and became septic. So whatever happened to me, once the pressure was relieved, I seem to have recovered well enough.

The story that Claudia Mullen tells is appalling, far worse than anything I remember. If her memories are accurate, then there is a monstrous evil in our midst that needs to be addressed by a morally committed government. But we don't have that, so my assumption is that the problem will continue to be ignored.

Her testimony was brushed aside by the Human Radiation Commission, and no further investigation took place. Essentially, she was dismissed as a fantasist, even though Valerie Wolf testified that "all of her memories have emerged spontaneously, without the use of memory enhancement techniques such as hypnosis or sodium amytal." She had been told nothing about government or CIA research projects by the counselor.

Two things happened after the Wolf-Mullen testimony. First was the formation of the Advocacy Committee for Human Experimentation Survivors, which went nowhere. The second was the creation of the False Memory Syndrome Foundation. Whether it was inspired by that testimony I do not know, but its validity was significantly compromised when Harvard psychologist Jennifer J. Freyd, the daughter of two of its founders, accused them of having abused her as a child in her book *Betrayal Trauma: The Logic of Forgetting Childhood Abuse*. Her book sought to reveal a mechanism for the suppression of traumatic memories, which the False Memory Syndrome Foundation maintains cannot exist.

Additionally, Dr. Freyd claims that Ralph Unterwager, who was also involved in the creation of the foundation, said of pedophilia in a June of 1991 interview in the Dutch publication *Paedika: The Journal of Paedophilia* that "certainly it is responsible." He continued, "Pedophiles spend a lot of time and energy defending their choice. I don't think that a pedophile needs to do that. Pedophiles can boldly and courageously affirm what they choose."

Hollida Wakefield, who remains involved with the False Memory Syndrome Foundation, said in the same publication, "It would be nice if someone could get some kind of big research grant to do a longitudinal study of, let's say, a hundred twelve year old boys in relationships with loving pedophiles."

In itself, this statement doesn't suggest anything about Dr. Wakefield other than an interest in the outcomes of pedophilic experiences, and Dr. Unterwager claimed that his part of the interview was taken out of context, but the fact remains that the False Memory Syndrome Foundation was founded by a couple associated with accusations of familial pedophilia by their daughter, herself a distinguished psychologist, and two psychologists whose words appeared in a publication that advocated pedophilia as a valid life choice.

The foundation has on its board numerous prominent scientists, including members of the National Science Foundation and Michael Persinger of Laurentian University, who has claimed to have induced paranormal experiences in test subjects using electromagnetic coils attached to a bicycle helmet, and who attributes UFOs to tectonic pressure. He explains the fact that UFOs are routinely observed and recorded in areas without tectonic activity with the claim that the effect can travel "hundreds of miles" before it generates any manifestations in the sky.

The False Memory Syndrome Foundation has more than enough authority to communicate its assertions effectively, and to turn aside any investigation into such uncomfortable subjects as possible abusive experiments on children, especially when the claims made are bizarre, as are many that you find on the Internet, and may involve recovered memory.

Personally, I cannot imagine how anybody who endured experiences as atrocious as Ms. Mullen recounts could possibly hope to describe them with any accuracy, especially while attempting to draw them out of the desperate confusion and fear of an abused childhood.

I had not suppressed my own memories. There's no sense that I forgot them. But I did ignore them until I suddenly ended up at Randolph, largely because they were extremely disturbing and had no context into which I could fit them into my life.

The only thing that is going to resolve the question of whether or not there has been, or still is, officially sanctioned abuse of children for scientific and national security reasons is documentation, but I would be very surprised if any will ever be forthcoming.

Before World War II, the U.S. government had acquired over the years a profound moral distinction. Sadly, however, the horrors of Nazism and the long struggle of the Cold War have left us with a vast secret bureaucracy concealed behind a veil of traditional institutions such as congress and the executive, which it dominates and manipulates at will.

However unconscionable it might have been to allow the Central Intelligence Agency to suppress the Finders investigation, it was done, and, in the end, no member of congress sufficiently powerful to oppose the CIA was willing to make the necessary demands.

Of course, I'm no one to talk. I'm just an "alien abductee," a fantasist without the slightest claim to credibility. Against a phalanx of distinguished professors and members of the National Academy of Sciences, my word and my testimony are without value, and are doomed to be ignored just as was the testimony given to the Clinton commission by Claudia Mullen.

I suspect that the victims claiming officially sanctioned child abuse have a story to tell that has not been told, and that they deserve that it be told, and in the telling, to obtain what healing might be afforded them.

However, in my estimation, what happened to me did not have an exclusively negative impact on my life.

In shattering the mirror of expectation for me, it opened my mind to a hidden reality that has greatly enriched me.

Had I not as a child been brutalized by whoever this was, I don't think that I ever would have been able to perceive the visitors. I would never have had the chance to do the impossible, which is to have formed a relationship with them.

Because I was so shocked in my childhood, I lost my belief in the stability of the ordinary world. I live in a permanent state of unease, but also a permanent state of wonder.

Ask any close-encounter witness what is real. They will tell you at once, it isn't what you see around you. This world of pretense in which we live is just like a shattered childhood, a very different place than it appears.

We smile and pretend that all is well.

But all is not well.

CHAPTER 4

Going West

IN 1994, ANNE AND I LEFT OUR CABIN IN UPSTATE
New York for the last time. My relationship with our
visitors had changed over the years, becoming more
complex, in some senses more strained. But at the
same time I had discovered a radiant and unexpected human component that was and is one of the great joys of my life.

On our last night at the cabin, I had one of the most remarkable
and beautiful experiences of my life.

Now, as we left that place behind us forever, I felt at once deso-
late and deeply awed. A great passage of our lives had come to its
conclusion.

I had never imagined that there would be a last time. I had expected
to spend the rest of my life there.

Inwardly, I was in greater turmoil than I had ever known. Not even
the days after my 1985 encounter could equal this.

I had seen beyond the edge of the world. I had seen a whole new form of life and way of being human that has hitherto remained hidden.

The night before we left the cabin forever had been the greatest moment of my life to that date.

But now, as I turned down Route 209 for the last time, and that beloved spot, so sacred to me, slipped away behind us, I had to ask myself: Why had people stopped buying my books?

It was not my fault, I knew that, but that wasn't how it felt. If I had not persisted in my public advocacy, my writing career would have regained traction, and the economic disruption that caused us to lose our property wouldn't have happened.

But I couldn't stop, not then and not now. Anne and I have seen realities that are not normally seen, but which we both feel strongly are key to understanding the miracle of humanity and perhaps even to ensuring that man has a future. Morally, neither of us has a choice: we must bear witness.

Inevitably, I am sure, the reality that we have known will cease to be hidden, and mankind will finally begin what I suspect is the next phase of our journey, which only starts in the material world that we know now.

After I published *Communion*, I endured a years-long media barrage that, in the end, led too many people to turn away from my work. No matter how hard I tried, I could not shake the relentless characterization of me as an advocate for belief in alien contact. When the aliens didn't land, people simply tuned me out. It seemed as if the inertia obscuring the true question simply could not be overcome. What was so sad was that it was and is an exciting, vital question, so much more engaging than the alien folklore that has enshrouded it.

We moved to a small condominium we owned in my hometown of San Antonio, Texas.

Since we left upstate New York, some explosively powerful and remarkable events have taken place, but that last night at the cabin marked a fundamental change. What happened there would be the last and most magnificent "contact" experience. But not with aliens. My last visitor was human—or had been. As will be seen when I discuss him in more detail, perhaps the most compelling discovery I have made in all my journey is that there is more than one mystery here. We are not what we seem, we human beings.

From the next morning on, my encounters with creatures that appeared to be alien would be few. Now the human aspect of the experience would enter my life as never before, and I would discover the most wonderful thing: a human being is much more than we have yet dared to imagine. Much, much more.

But on that morning, I had barely even begun to process the meaning of what had transpired over the previous few years at the cabin, much less the epochal event that had taken place the night before.

As we drove down the highway on that sad morning, my cell phone rang. It was an old, dear friend, the filmmaker and photographer Timothy Greenfield-Sanders, who had been the first person I'd told about my 1985 encounter, even before I told Anne. I had decided to try the story on him and get his advice about how to tell my wife before I actually faced her with it.

Now he said, "Whitley, I just saw your woman, the woman on the cover of *Communion*. She came up to my car and leaned in the window while I was stuck in traffic on Fourteenth Street." He paused. "She's prettier than that picture."

My heart almost stopped. How I envied him. Now that I was leaving, maybe he was going to be my replacement.

Later, he also commented that her eyes were different from those in my picture. "They're hard to describe. Deep and dark, but not like dark glasses. You can see something in them."

I have always regretted that picture, because it communicates the idea of an alien presence far more forcefully than I had intended. But at the same time, the picture has served as a mnemonic for many people, who have, upon seeing it, realized that their own encounters were not simply ordinary dreams.

On that morning, he continued, "She asked me if I was going west. I said, 'No, I'm going east,' and she said, 'Well, that's good.'"

I knew exactly what this meant. She was not only expressing gladness that Timothy was staying but also regret at my departure.

I might add here that while it may seem extraordinary that somebody who appears even slightly like her could walk the streets of a crowded city, she could and did. Up close, there was something deeply human about her. One did not get an impression so much of alien as of human strangeness, and the feeling that one was face-to-face with a living aspect of a very deep mystery, which is the mystery of man.

As I reported in *Transformation*, immediately after *Communion* was published she and another such being showed up in the old Madison Avenue Bookshop in Manhattan while Bruce Lee, an editor from my publisher, William Morrow, was checking the stock. He saw them paging quickly through *Communion* and drew closer. They were laughing about the various things I'd gotten wrong. Then they stopped and looked up at Bruce. When he saw their eyes, he was unable to remain near them and left the store.

I know that it will seem completely incredible that such people could go unnoticed in public, but I have no reason to doubt either of these witnesses, and when I challenged Mr. Lee, he took a polygraph to support his claim, and passed it.

In February of 2004, a city councilor in Winchester in England had an extraordinary sighting. Councilor Adrian Hicks reported that "I was near The Works bookshop when I saw this strange woman, a humanoid walking with a penguinlike gait. She had very large prominent eyes and was twirling her hands in a circular motion."

I interviewed Mr. Hicks, who was completely straightforward about his description of this being. She was wearing an odd, frilly dress and had long hair and was unmistakably not human. She also seemed perfectly happy and at ease as she strolled down the street. He told me that people walked past her without noticing, and that he still believes that somebody else must surely have seen her and that he hopes they will come forward.

When I hung up the phone, I recognized that I was saying good-bye to one kind of life, and heading off into an unknown life that certainly did not seem promising.

But the next few years would be marked by a whole new level of experience.

I would meet William Mallow of the Southwest Research Institute and at last see scientific investigation of some of the physical materials involved in the close encounter and UFO experiences. I would continue to have experiences, most of them of a very new kind, culminating, in June of 1998, with an encounter of overwhelming awe and wonder, and deep humanity.

That wasn't what I was anticipating as we left for Texas, though. I was in a state of shock. I couldn't believe that sales of my books had fallen off a cliff. I couldn't believe that we'd come to this. I couldn't believe that the magnificent experience I'd had on that last night was behind me forever.

But it wasn't behind me. Far from it. In fact, nothing was at an end. I was, at most, midway along the path that I now know will not end even with death.

But the fact remained that we had just moved from a lovely home on a hundred and fifty acres of magic-filled woods to a tiny two-bedroom condo in a nondescript corner of north San Antonio—a couple of miles from the elegant neighborhood where I'd grown up, and where most of my childhood friends, all now far more successful than me, still lived.

The difference was so stark that even my wife, who is normally rather indifferent to social matters, felt an acute sense of humiliation. I could well understand this, because I felt it myself. But there was nothing to be done except soldier on and be glad we still had a roof over our heads.

Going from our isolated cabin to this urban environment, I assumed that I would never see the visitors again, but this turned out not to be the case. We had not been in the condo complex but for a few weeks when the being on the cover of *Communion* put in another appearance.

During the last year of our time in upstate New York, a number of local people had encountered the visitors while on our property. Once, some workmen had quit pulling poison ivy out of our trees after seeing what their foreman described as "an alien" walking across our access road, and there had been other instances as well.

Many locals found the whole subject frightening, and in the summer of 1994, we began receiving ominous phone calls. A female voice would say not to go out in the woods during the next hunting season, because somebody was planning for me to be the victim of an "accident." Once, when I brought the groceries home, I discovered that somebody had at some point spit in one of the bags. Somebody had also been defecating in the circle of stones I had built at the site of my 1985 encounter.

I accepted all of this as more or less inevitable. In fact, I was surprised it hadn't happened earlier. People fear the unknown, and our world is still dominated to a very great degree by superstition. Many people assume that there can only be angels, men, and demons, and I don't think it ever occurs to any of them that I might be in league with angels.

So the hostility didn't surprise me, and I assumed that the danger we were in was quite real. Even so, we hated to give up the cabin, and when we got to the little apartment in San Antonio and Anne saw what she had, she cried. But she also set about doing what she has always done, which was to make it into a nice home, and soon the two small bedrooms and living-dining room had become a comfortable nest for us, and I was writing again, hoping to make some money.

There was just one problem. We were not alone. We had been followed.

The previous August, I had been walking one afternoon in the woods when I had seen what looked to me like a boy of perhaps eleven sitting under a tree, smoking. He was on my property, which was bad enough, but worse, he was about twenty yards from a stand of pitch pines, which, on a hot day in a dry summer, are virtual bombs.

I went over to him to ask him to be careful, but when I leaned down, I got a shock. This was no boy, but it wasn't a man, either. He looked like somebody who had ceased to age before puberty, and was now not a man but a sort of weathered child.

Staring straight ahead, he made a low sound. It was ominous enough to send me heading back to the cabin, and fast.

I realized that we'd been smelling cigarette smoke in and near the cabin for some time. We don't smoke and there were no other houses close by, so it had been a bit troubling, but not enough to really get on my radar.

Our swimming pool was very private, so Anne and I on occasion used to go skinny-dipping. When we did it a few days later, somebody started running up and down in the woods behind the yard, gasping and cracking sticks. The quick steps indicated short stature, and I had a feeling I knew who this was.

We went inside immediately, of course. I threw my clothes on, grabbed my shotgun, and tore out after the intruder.

This was all I needed: a sinister chain-smoking dwarf hiding out behind the house and watching us.

I tried to track him down, but without success. I found a number of places where he must have lingered, because they were littered with cigarette butts. We also began hearing odd sounds in the woods both day and night.

This, coupled with the threats and the growing sense of local hostility, made the stop my late-night walks on which much of my experience had depended. It didn't matter, though. As I will discuss later, my life with the visitors had already changed in a very surprising way, and was now routinely unfolding right in the house. I hadn't needed to go into the woods anymore.

So the house was being watched by a strange sort of boy-man who chain-smoked. Writing this today, in 2010, it sounds as droll as it was fantastic, but at the time it was extremely worrying. We were alone back in that cabin. Of course I was armed and the place was loaded with electronic protection and lights, but still, I felt that we were very vulnerable.

I had not been nearly as frightened of the gray, apparently alien creatures as I was of human beings.

But what was this creature? He had obviously been worried when we were skinny-dipping, so he seemed not to be a danger, but what was he?

I decided to think of him as a sort of guardian. He seemed to be there day and night, and no matter the weather. I must have tried getting a photo of him a dozen times, including a number of sessions of just shooting at random, but I was, as usual, not successful.

The cabin had been isolated, but the condo in Texas was at street level in an urban neighborhood. There was nowhere in the area to hide. The nearest woods were in the Olmos Basin two miles away. So when I smelled cigarette smoke one night, I assumed that I was experiencing another of the difficulties of living in close quarters, and for a few nights I continued to assume that there was a smoker living nearby. But then a neighbor across from us mentioned something odd. A child had been noticed in the complex doing strange things. It was a boy who looked about twelve. He'd been seen climbing the wall of one of the buildings. The occupants of the second-story condo he'd been climbing toward had found the spokes torn out of their bicycle tires.

There was no way anybody could have climbed that wall. Unfortunately, my neighbor didn't know who had seen this, but I was able to talk to the couple whose bikes had been vandalized. They were completely mystified. They had been at work when it happened. They couldn't imagine who had done it or why.

Cigarette smoke. Strange feral child who could climb walls and did things that were faintly ominous and inexplicable—but no, it was impossible. We'd left all that behind in upstate New York.

The cigarette smoke continued to bother us in our bedroom, and one night I stepped quickly out onto the porch just in time to see a short figure dart out of the cul-de-sac beside it.

My suspicions were confirmed: it was him.

So now I was certain: this was no ordinary child. Somehow, he had followed us from upstate New York.

Was he still guarding us, then? I thought we'd surely left the danger behind, but that may not have been entirely true.

A short time before he showed up, a strange incident had taken place. I had been resting in the bedroom of our condo one afternoon when I'd suddenly heard a male voice threatening to kidnap me. Of course I was terrified and I leaped up. As the voice had sounded like it was inside my head, by the time I was on my feet, I assumed that it had been a nightmare. But then I saw two men standing just outside the porch. I ran outside yelling, and they turned, obviously shocked, and dashed down to the street. They got into a black car and drove away.

However they had communicated their threat I do not know, but it was extremely menacing.

I don't think it was more than a few days later that I began to notice the cigarette smoke, and then to be aware of our guardian in the cul-de-sac.

The two individuals who had threatened me did not reappear, but the strange man stood out there night after night, until finally I could stand it no longer. I installed a motion-sensitive light in the space he was using.

All the next night, it went on and off, on and off. Each time, I rushed out, camera in hand, but each time saw nothing.

The night after that was quiet. No cigarette smoke, no light turning on and off. Later that morning, I was working in the small garden that was part of the condo, and situated between the porch and the street.

Suddenly, he came bursting out of the alley and went marching off down the street. He looked absolutely furious. He had a cigarette sticking out of the center of his mouth.

I called to him, then got up and went after him. He kept his distance, moving faster and faster. I watched him stomp off down the street.

I have never seen him since.

I have wondered, though. I have wondered and wondered. Did he bring the danger with him, or was he trying to protect us? Who was he? And, above all, *what*?

Finally, I had to add him to the vast question that is my life. But I have thought long about where he might have gone, and what his experience of life might be. He is somewhere, I feel sure, in the deeps of this mysterious world of ours.

I found my hometown reaching out to me in ways that no other community ever had. With the publication of *Communion*, all but a few of our friends in New York had evaporated, but San Antonio did not reject me.

In 1988, local reporter Ed Conroy had written a book about me called *Report on Communion* that had helped to establish my credibility and made it impossible for the propagandists and fake skeptics who feed on UFO subjects to dismiss me as a charlatan.

Soon after arriving, we met Catherine Cooke, the director of a local organization called the Mind Science Foundation. It had been founded by her uncle, a wealthy oilman and adventurer called Tom Slick, whom I had met a few times as a boy. Mr. Slick had organized, in 1954, the first scientific expedition in search of the yeti. He had also founded the Southwest Research Institute.

Cathy upheld the spirit of adventure that her uncle had championed, and I was invited to speak before the Mind Science Foundation.

Not only that, Anne was welcomed into our family, into the large group of friends we had there, and into the reading club that my great-grandmother had helped to found more than a hundred years previously, in which all the women in my family have participated for generations.

The social silence of New York was ended, and she found herself part of a wide group of friends again.

I was also eager to work with Bill Mallow. With his vast knowledge of materials and the array of superb equipment at his disposal, I anticipated that some of the little objects that had been removed from people would be interesting subjects for analysis. Also, in May of 1989, I had experienced the placement of such an object in my own body.

I was awake when it happened, and I remembered every detail of the event. My experience with this object, and the fantastic result of the attempt to remove it that took place in 1994, are the subject of the next chapter of this book.

In 1994 and 1995, Bill and I had little to work on—a couple of supposed implants, but analysis proved inconclusive, insofar as the materials were extremely unusual but not necessarily unearthly. Of course, at the time, we were looking exclusively for objects that we could prove were of non-earth origin. In retrospect, we might have been looking at a smoking gun without realizing it: two of the objects we studied were highly unusual but, we assumed, made here. One was a sliver of crystalline glass called sital, which came out of the leg of a boy. Another was a fragment that had turned up in the mail of radio host Art Bell, which turned out to be an amalgam of layered magnesium and bismuth. The magnesium had been made into a foam. How, exactly, this material held together, or for what use it would have been manufactured, we could not determine.

I still had the object in my ear, and was still unsure of what to do about it. From time to time, it would turn my ear bright red and make a rough staticlike sound, and I really wanted Bill to witness this before I had it removed. But there was no way to predict when it would happen, so I waited, hoping for the best.

Then the flow of materials increased. In 1996, Dr. Roger Leir, a California podiatric surgeon, was shown an X-ray of an implant at a UFO conference he had attended at the instigation of a friend. He was intrigued enough to remove it, and he found that it was, oddly enough, encased in skin. This had fooled the host's body into not rejecting it. But we have no genetic encoding that enables skin to grow inside deep muscle tissue, so unless it was created surgically, the encasement was completely inexplicable. But we also don't have surgical techniques that would enable us to do such a thing.

In any case, the object soon ended up under Bill's microscope, as did a number of others that Dr. Leir and the general surgeons who worked with him had collected.

As of this writing, sixteen objects have been removed from close-encounter witnesses. Six of them were found to be emitting radio signals while in situ. The radio frequencies were: 8 Hz, 17 MHz, 110 MHz, 1.2 GHz, 137.72926 MHz, and 516.812 GHz.

The objects that Dr. Leir gave to Bill for testing were uniformly almost pure iron, usually with a trace of nickel and other metals in their composition. Generally, they were unremarkable, and there was nothing to prove that they might be anything from another world.

One, however, presented an extraordinary puzzle to us. This was the first object that had ever been found to be emitting a radio signal prior to its removal from a witness's body. We had hoped to find some sign of circuitry or some sort of crystalline formation in the object that might explain the radio signal. But it was as unremarkable as the others.

Finally, we took it to the University of Texas at San Antonio, where there was an X-ray diffraction instrument. The hope was that we might be able to detect something inside the object using X-ray diffraction. At this point, we knew that the object was 99 percent pure iron.

As recorded in my 1999 NBC special *Confirmation*, when we placed the object in the diffractor, for the first few seconds it returned a signal, as would be expected from iron. But then the diffractor ceased to return any signal at all. It was as if the object had been removed.

We ran it for a time, then checked the diffractor against known objects. It was in normal working order. Still, the implant remained X-ray invisible. We then returned it to the scanning electron microscope and got the same result as before: 99 percent pure iron.

It was left in X-ray diffraction for another thirty-six hours but never returned another signal. What mechanism might have enabled it to become X-ray invisible is unknown.

Further study would have gone beyond the scope of what we could do at Southwest Research, so the object was returned to Dr. Leir. To my knowledge, there has been no further study of this object, and its secrets remain intact. Unfortunately, the lack of funding for this sort of research is, to say the least, absolute.

I have often wondered about the strange mix of technological sophistication and primitive miniaturization that characterizes the implants. We can make radio-frequency-identification devices that are the size of particles of dust. So why would supposedly advanced aliens be using things that were as large as these? Frankly, I would have dismissed them as natural objects, had it not been for the fact that I have watched the sheathing of epidermis being dissected away from them, and observed the radio scanner picking up their signals.

Are they meant to be found? To cause us to question them?

Those are questions about which we can, at present, only speculate.

In any case, when Bill Mallow and I were working with them, we were thrilled by the scientific adventure we were on. With his superb knowledge of materials and all the wonderful equipment he had access to, it felt as if we were on the brink of some major discoveries.

Until, suddenly, it was all brought to a halt.

After the *Confirmation* special aired on NBC, Bill said to me that he would no longer be able to do voluntary work with us. As matters stood, he had been able to provide reports only on plain paper, usually handwritten, or verbal reports. He said that the director of SWRI had told him that their CIA client, which was responsible for nearly half their budget, took a "dim view" of UFO research and didn't want it to be done on the campus at all.

Whether he had really been told this by a CIA representative, we didn't know and couldn't find out, but Bill obviously did not wish to jeopardize the institution's standing with its most important client, so that was basically the end of our research.

In 2002, Bill died, and I lost the best scientist, I believe, who has ever examined these mysterious objects.

From what I have seen, though, I believe that the implants are genuine mysteries. But I have another reason to believe this, too, which is that in May of 1989, while I was wide awake, I was myself implanted. Not only that, the object that was inserted under the skin of my left ear—without leaving the slightest trace of an entry point on the skin—was put there not by strange creatures but by two quite ordinary-appearing people.

I saw them as they ran toward me across the bedroom. I will never forget them, or what happened on that soft May night, as I was plunged more deeply than ever into the mysterious experience that has so completely consumed my life.

CHAPTER 5
My Implant

THE IDEA THAT SOMEONE UNKNOWN MIGHT be implanting strange technological objects in human beings is so frightening that to many people it is literally infuriating. Often, it is rejected out of hand, purely on emotional grounds.

That this is happening may be unwanted information, but it is long past time to face it. What these objects do is a matter for careful study.

By May of 1989, I had lost interest in implants. An MRI study we had done of a number of people claiming implants in their nasal cavities had returned no results. This suggested to me—thankfully—that they were probably just another aspect of the intricate folklore that has grown up around the close-encounter phenomenon. It would still be years before I met Bill Mallow or heard of Dr. Roger Leir.

My personal confrontation with implants came on a warm night, late in the month. The windows of our bedroom, which overlooked the driveway, were open.

In those days, I did not sleep well at all, especially not during the small hours of the night. Usually, I would drop into a deeper sleep right around dawn. But in the small hours of the morning, I was, if not wide awake, then only lightly asleep.

On that night, I heard a very distinct and immediately recognizable sound: the crunching of gravel in the driveway. It was easy to hear. The night was still and dead quiet.

It could mean only one thing: there was a vehicle out there. I'd seen no car lights reflected on the ceiling. Therefore, it had approached with its lights out.

My worst fear, by that time, was not being assaulted by strange beings. My fear was assault by people. Later, things would get even worse, but already by 1989 I was feeling a distinct atmosphere of hostility from the local community.

As I went from my half-asleep state to full wakefulness, I heard a male voice in the backyard say "Condition red."

That did it. No question: we were under threat.

I had prepared carefully for this. Beside the bed was a bank of switches that would flood the area around the house with light. Under my bed were two firearms: a .45 automatic and a Benelli M2 Tactical Riot Gun, and I was well practiced on both of these formidable weapons.

As I reached for the switches, a terrific shock went through me. There were people right here, right in the room.

I saw a man and a woman standing in the doorway at the far end of the bedroom. I shifted my focus, going instead for the shotgun. Had I succeeded in getting it into my hands, I would absolutely have blown them away.

For an instant, they stood frozen. The woman was in front. She was perhaps five-foot-seven, with long, straight hair. Like the man behind her, she wore a black bodysuit of some kind. The man was much larger, easily taller than six feet, and had a beard. Behind him, there may have been additional movement, but I have never been sure.

As I turned to my left, reaching downward toward the gun, they arrived beside the bed.

The next thing I knew, I was lying on my right side and there were waves of pressure being applied to the left side of my head. The woman was speaking softly.

This continued on for some little time, perhaps as long as two or three minutes. I felt as if my mind had been detached from my body. I willed my legs to kick, my fists to swing, but nothing happened. It wasn't like being paralyzed, not exactly. It was more as if my body was under the control of someone else, and it was a very odd sensation, quite unlike what I imagine paralysis to be. It wasn't that I couldn't move, but rather that when my mind commanded my body to move, nothing happened.

I could no longer see. My eyes weren't closed that I was aware, but all I could perceive was blackness.

The pushing against my temple came in waves, pressing my head down into the pillow again and again. The woman's voice continued to murmur softly.

Suddenly I heard a great crashing in the woods, and found that I could sit up and I could see. A huge flash of light came in the windows but was gone in an instant.

I leaped out of bed and went for my switches. My own floodlights revealed an empty driveway on one side of the house and an empty pool deck and garden on the other.

The alarm system was armed, its red LED glowing steadily.

I grabbed the Benelli and went through the house, starting in the basement and working my way up into the attic. I checked every door and window, looked under every bed and into every closet.

There was nobody in the house. There was no sign of activity outside.

I returned to the bedroom and put the gun back under the bed. As had happened so often before, I was left without any clear idea of whether or not this had been some sort of nightmare.

I stayed awake for a long time, listening to every rustle of a leaf, every sigh of a breeze, but all remained still and quiet. When dawn came, I got about an hour of sleep.

At about seven, Anne stirred. As I had so often, I asked her if she remembered anything unusual during the night. She just laughed and went on about her business.

I showered and dressed, and, as always, went out to the garage, planning to go down to the little store in town and buy the newspaper.

To my amazement, though, I found the garage door wide open.

The alarm system was still on, the red LED glowing normally.

I stared at the open door. I looked back at the alarm panel. Then I input the code and watched as the LED changed to green.

Something was clearly amiss here. I knew how the alarm system worked. For it not to have been tripped by the opening of that door, it would have had to have been rewired while the system was disarmed. If the switch was tripped while the system was armed and had either main power or battery backup, the alarm had to sound.

The door was open, so the switch was tripped. The alarm had not sounded.

Never quick to decide that the impossible was real, I got in the car, still intent on my habitual morning errand. As I backed out, though, I found that the car was full of static electricity, to the extent that it popped and crackled against my palms as I moved them on the steering wheel.

Afraid that the car was going to explode, I jumped out. I went inside and immediately called the alarm man.

When he came, he discovered that there was a very powerful magnetic field around the switch. I could see it registering on his magnetometer.

There was no way that it could be accounted for, but it was what had prevented the switch from triggering the alarm when the door was opened. The switch had to be replaced.

We also tried to dump the alarm system's records, but the dates were not set correctly, so we couldn't be sure if any entries had been recorded the previous night.

Only then was I certain that the incident had really happened.

One would think that by that time I would just accept such things, but that was far from the case. Despite a lifetime of strange experiences— or perhaps because of it—I have an almost relentless need to reject them. I don't want to be barraged by the inexplicable. I don't want to be involved with visitors, implants, UFOs, or any of the rest of it.

I set out to be a writer and lead a quiet life. I wanted enough sales to support my family, and I hoped for the approval of my peers. I wanted to contribute to the literary culture.

The last thing I wanted life to bring me was this unending sense of rejection, and the feeling that I'm considered either a charlatan or a lunatic, especially when what I have to offer is potentially so important and so valuable.

I didn't want to believe that what I remembered had really happened. And, even more, I didn't want to believe what happened next.

Later that day, I noticed a sore lump at the top of my left ear. There was no trace of a scar or a wound, just the hard lump, red and sore.

As I stood in the bathroom, feeling it, trying to see it, a wave of helpless rage overcame me. My first impulse was to get a blade and dig it out. But as I went through my tool kit, searching for razor blades, another thought intruded: *This is real, and it means something. It is there for a reason, and if I stay calm, maybe I can determine that reason.*

I remembered how violated I'd felt the morning after the 1985 encounter, and the sense of flesh-crawling horror that had come over me a few days later, when the rectal injury I had sustained became apparent. Then, I felt dirty, so dirty that I washed and washed.

This was different. I remembered the way the two people had

looked, and the soft kindness of the woman's voice. I don't think that she'd been speaking, but rather humming softly. She had been trying to comfort me, that was very clear.

God, though, I did feel like a lab rat.

What if this thing was going to control my mind? What in the name of *God* was it going to do?

To be honest, I came close to cutting my own ear off. But then I thought, *I'm like a dog chewing at a suture, too damn ignorant to know that it's there for my own good.*

Except, was it?

For the first few nights after it was placed, I meditated as usual. Nothing happened. My days were spent in the increasingly desperate attempt to keep my financial head above water. The long failure was just beginning in 1989, which would lead to the loss of the cabin five years later. I still had hope. Confidence. And an implant in my ear.

Who were those people?

One night, perhaps a week after the implantation, I was startled by a flash of imagery in my head while I was meditating. It went past fast, but it seemed like a picture of the interior of a room. I'd had some vivid imagery before, which I have reported in *Communion* and the follow-on books, but nothing as bright as this.

Too fast, though.

From time to time, the ear would get red and hot, and I would hear a strange rasping sound in it.

Of course, I kept Anne informed about everything I was thinking and feeling and experiencing, and she was in favor of my leaving it in. I could always get it taken out later.

In retrospect, I'm glad that I followed her advice, because of the crucial events that unfolded over the next few years. I was destined to have two towering experiences, and, while I cannot know if the implant facilitated them, it didn't prevent them.

When the first of these experiences started, I resolved to leave the object in place at least until what was actually a whole new level of close encounter ended. What happened was that people, not aliens, began to show up while I was meditating. They were physical but had capabilities very unlike our own. Among other things, they could appear and disappear at will. Meditating with them was among the most powerful experiences I have ever had. It fundamentally changed my understanding of reality, opening my mind to what has become for me a fundamental truth: we do not see the world around us as it really is. It is vastly more complex, more alive, and more conscious than we imagine.

In a later chapter, I will detail exactly what happened at the cabin in the years after I got the implant. I would not trade those years for anything. Not for anything. I learned what it really means to be human, that existence is not confined to the strange interlude between birth and death but is something altogether more dynamic, a grand, serious, and extremely complex state, of which those of us in the physical perceive only a small part.

So on one level it appeared that the implant was taking the adventure of my life to new heights, granting sight to a man who had, without even knowing it, been blind. On another level, though, I had the sense that I might no longer be free. It used to wake me up in the sweated night, and I would sit on the bedside feeling the thing and wondering if it was a mechanism of freedom or a chain of slavery.

When we lived in upstate New York, though, I couldn't think who might be willing to remove it. Dr. Leir had yet to do his first surgery. The study I'd done had failed, and I was no longer in touch with the doctor who had run it. My GP had taken one look at it, laughed, and said, "What do you think it is, an alien implant?" I'd explained that it had gotten irritated when I slept on it. He said that if it got irritated again to come back and he'd look at it then.

So I went on, bearing it in my body, worrying about it, wanting to jump out of my own skin to get away from it.

I was never at peace with it, not from the beginning, and when we moved to Texas, I resolved to finally find a doctor who would take it out.

But first I took another bank of psychological tests, similar to the ones I'd taken after the Communion experience. I wanted to see if there had been any changes in my mental state that might stem from its presence in my body. I suppose that I was looking for some evidence of mind control, but standard psychological tests are designed to evaluate one's mental state and detect pathology, not to reveal something like that.

In any case, the results were the same as always: I was living at an extremely high level of stress but was otherwise normal.

I decided to take matters a step beyond where they were and actually spend some time in analysis with a psychologist. I found one who was willing to let her professional neutrality guide her when it came to explanations for the close encounters. I didn't want somebody who would try to fit them into existing definitions of pathology, and I certainly didn't want a believer.

I met Elizabeth Lerman, who had a thriving and successful practice in Kerrville, Texas, concentrating on abused children. During the year I spent consulting with her, she never expressed an opinion about the close-encounter phenomenon. To this day, I have no idea what she thinks of it.

She was a specialist in childhood trauma, and did think that a lot of my stress could be traced back to something that had gone amiss in my childhood. I did not tell her the story of Randolph in the same way that I have told it here, because at the time I was still piecing it together.

Initially, I told her nothing about the implant. What I was attempting to do was see if she thought there might be some outside influence affecting my mental processes. If I told her I had an implant in my ear and was worried about mind control, I thought that she would probably diagnose me as a paranoid and proceed on that basis.

She did think that the childhood memories I described suggested that I had been abused when very small. Specifically, she was rather certain that the memory of being taken to the camp counselor's house and trapped by the strange man was an incident of abuse that had been facilitated by the counselor.

I did mention the implant to Bill Mallow. One day when we were together in his office, I told him the story of the implantation. Rather remarkably—or perhaps by design—it turned on while I was telling him about it.

He saw the ear turn bright red. He felt the heat that was generated. He rushed me into a signals lab, but they were unable to detect any radio frequency coming from it.

I found a local doctor, John Lerma, who diagnosed the swelling as a probable benign cyst and agreed to take it out. He was aware of my books, but, unlike my upstate New York GP, he did not have any awareness of implants.

For the next few days, I wondered what would happen when it was gone. Would I be relieved? Desolated?

On the day of the appointment, Anne and I went to Dr. Lerma's office, video camera in hand. He agreed that we could tape the surgery.

As he prepared to remove it, he determined that it was fixed in the pinna of my ear, close to the top. He marked it, then washed the ear and anesthetized it.

As he began the dissection, Anne taped the proceedings, all the while talking nervously. I think we were all a bit nervous. I certainly was. In fact, inside myself, I was in turmoil. As Dr. Lerma opened the incision more and more, I would feel a slight pressure against my ear. He narrated what he was seeing. He fell silent for a moment, then reported, "It's a white disk." Anne and his nurse could see it too.

He started to draw it out—and the impossible happened. The thing moved, and not just slightly. Despite the fact that it had appeared so fixed in place that he thought it must be embedded in the cartilage, it became mobile and slid under the skin from the top of my ear down into my earlobe.

Understand, this actually happened. While the tape we made doesn't show the movement, it does show the reactions of the people observing, including Dr. Lerma, who has spoken about the event publicly many times.

There isn't anything in nature that would do that, not a random particle that had somehow gotten under my skin, not a cyst, not any known parasite.

Dr. Lerma elected not to continue the surgery, saying that he could not proceed without maiming me, which was obviously quite true. So he pulled out and stitched up the wound. But he had also gotten a sliver of the object on his instrument when he touched it. This he put in a stable solution in order to send it to pathology.

With the rest of the object now floating in my earlobe, I went home.

That night, I lay awake until late hours, touching my ear again and again. There it was, still there in the earlobe.

But how, and why? Had it moved away from the scalpel because removing it would harm me, or to protect itself, or for the sake of both of us?

What questions surged through my mind in those long, difficult hours. Always, I had thought to myself that in the end I would get it removed, but now I felt captured by it. I was the prisoner of this thing, and of the people who had put it into my body.

Two days later, I was sitting in the living room, reading, when I suddenly felt an acute burning sensation in the ear. I reached up, gingerly touching the bandage, then the earlobe.

The object had moved back into the top of my ear and was now situated where it remains to this day, right under the suture that Dr. Lerma had made in the removal attempt.

A couple of days after the surgery, the pathologist telephoned Dr. Lerma and told him that the fragment was the strangest thing he had ever seen. It consisted of a metallic base with organic cilia growing out of it. He did not believe it was anything natural, or that it was known technology.

So we had another unknown object, or a fragment of one, from my own body. To this day, the rest of it remains in place, and I remain unsure about it. I have no sense of being under any kind of control, or having my mind influenced in any way. But how would I know?

Not a day of my life passes that I don't wonder about the implant and the people who put it in me. *People*, two of them, perhaps more in the hallway behind them. They entered the house using a magnetic technology advanced enough to site a free-floating magnetic field that could neutralize an alarm system and then remain in place for hours.

Magnetic fields are generated by magnets. They don't simply appear out of nowhere. But this one did.

They implanted the thing in my ear in such a way that there was no external wound, and the object has extremely unusual properties.

So who were they? Where did they come from? What is their knowledge of life? What are their aims?

I was left mystified, and as I reach up and feel the object, I still am.

To this day, it occasionally turns on.

I do not doubt the implants. How can I, given that I harbor one?

These objects are physically real and a genuine mystery. There is no sane way to deny this, so, instead, they are ignored. But can it be wise to pretend that such an intimate intrusion into the human body isn't happening, merely because it is intimidating and frightening?

It is worth considering what they might be for. First, it cannot be assumed that because the signals some of them emit are weak they cannot be detected at a distance. We have no idea what these signals might be doing, if anything. For it is possible that the implants are not there to track people, to influence their thoughts or their bodies, but for reasons that might be beyond our science. My own experience suggests to me that this could be true. But there is yet another reason.

I have spoken with a number of people who have had theirs removed, and some have felt a sense of loss, in one case, "as if some part of me has died," while others have felt in some deep way set free.

Right now, the whole matter of UFOs, close encounters, implants, and everything that goes with them is in need not of the right answers but the right questions, and we will not even begin to reach them until we are well into analysis of the physical evidence.

Although I have devoted my search to finding the right questions, I cannot become ensnared in it. The implants are physically real, and searching for reasons why they cannot be real and therefore are not worthy of study is the exact opposite of what we should be doing, but it will be the first thing that leaps to mind for people who find them too disturbing to face, in particular, scientists and intellectuals who like to see themselves as the initiating and controlling figures in our culture.

I find it hard to bear, as I reach toward the last decades of my life, that I live in a society that cannot simply face facts and begin to address them in the sort of competent and organized manner that is necessary to making sense of them.

Instead we go on pretending. Any evidence suggesting, at any level, that the profound intrusion we see all around us is real must be wrong, probably faked outright or at least misconstrued. So we dismiss it.

Admittedly, the evidence of implants has not been developed to the highest level of finish, but from what has been done, it is crystal clear that more study is warranted. Not only that, Dr. Leir has many cases that he has been unable to examine for lack of money and support. And behind those there must be many more, but nobody can know for sure because of the social dangers that close-encounter witnesses face, especially those who are in vulnerable situations, such as scientists and academics.

Both Dr. Leir and the deceased Harvard psychiatrist Dr. John Mack, who did serious and open-minded work with close-encounter witnesses, experienced attacks on their professional credentials because of their interest in the subject. To his credit, the man who most aggressively attacked Dr. Mack, attempting to get his license to practice medicine and his tenure revoked, was open-minded enough to look at the evidence he had amassed that close encounters were a genuine unknown, and ceased his attacks. Dr. Leir defeated the attack on his credentials more conventionally, by proving that he remained competent to engage in his profession.

If there were not seventeen proven implants but ten thousand, then there could be some amazing research done. A record of the radio frequencies in use could be gathered. The witnesses could receive extensive physical and psychological examinations. Their narratives could be gathered and, using fMRI scanning techniques, it could be determined just how their brains functioned as they related those narratives. There is no question but that interesting data could be gathered, and maybe with it some answers.

I am often asked what I think of "disclosure." Will the president ever tell the truth about the UFO situation?

Frankly, I don't think so, and one of the reasons is the information presented in this chapter. If a president were to say even that some few unidentified flying objects appearing in our skies might be directed by an unknown intelligence, people with implants are going to come forward, and it won't be long before the press is screaming that aliens are here and they're putting strange objects in our bodies.

What governmental entity is ever going to admit that it has failed so profoundly at its most fundamental task, which is to protect its citizens? So I doubt that there will be disclosure, not unless the issue is forced by our visitors.

I raise my hand to my ear again and feel the little knot that has been part of me over these two decades. I remember the people who put it in me. But I also know just how very deceptive all of this is. And what of that voice saying "Condition red?" Why would somebody with their capabilities need to communicate vocally like that? They got past an armed alarm system. They froze my nervous system. They inserted a sophisticated object into my ear without leaving any wound.

And yet they apparently didn't even have radios. And why would my coming to consciousness be detected by somebody outside of the house instead of the people who were on the point of entering the bedroom? Any competent planner would have given them the device necessary to determine my state of consciousness. All they would have needed would be a dynamic cardioid microphone sensitive enough to pick up a heartbeat at a short distance and a small computer to interpret the sound and alert them if I was waking up.

Whatever this intelligence we are dealing with is, it has, by using things like the implants, very adroitly gained control over our own social and official response to its presence, and it has done this by placing our government in the impossible position of having to admit not only to a long history of deception but also that it is helpless to control what amounts to the most profound intrusion into individual lives that has ever happened.

Thus, even if the implants do nothing at all, they certainly serve as a means of social control. They ensure that our governments will keep the secrets of our visitors, if they are visitors.

It could be that the objects—easy to find, broadcasting mysterious signals, and offering ominous proof that our authorities do not have the situation under control—are meant to be discovered.

Let's imagine for a moment that we're the species with the ability to reach a planet bearing a less-advanced culture. We want to study them and eventually, when they are closer to us in their development, also meet them. But we notice that they are engaged in conflict among themselves. They're aggressive and ignorant but far from stupid.

When we attempt to communicate with them, the first thing they do is start shooting. What's worse, we're not prepared, some of our material gets shot down, and we end up leaving their best armed and most aggressive governing entity with certain knowledge that we are here. Perhaps they even capture some of us, or make off with the bodies of dead crew.

We need to fix this, and fast. Otherwise this entire species is going to become aware of us and direct its aggression toward us. Seeing our awesome technology, it is also going to become disempowered, cease to innovate on its own, and become a supplicant.

We need to gain control over their policy toward us, and to do that we will concentrate our efforts on the government that knows the most about us.

The best way to do that without taking any overt action would be to place it in the position of forcing it, if it reveals us, to also reveal its inability to control us.

Implants are a wonderfully elegant solution to the problem of unwanted disclosure. Our visitors don't need to threaten. Far from it. As long as the implants are there to reveal official helplessness, they can go about their business in complete confidence that the secrecy they need will be rigorously enforced—by the leadership of the very species that is under study and, conceivably, is also being exploited in some way.

Like everything our visitors do, this elegant and inexpensive solution accomplishes an enormous goal at very little cost to them.

But what is that goal? Why would they want secrecy in the first place?

Obviously, some of the possible reasons are ominous. Maybe they want to exploit us. Are doing so. How would be another question.

In the common narrative of close encounter, there is much material about them wanting to take what is usually referred to as "human DNA." There are also many reports of sexual material being taken. I would agree with these reports, because it happened to me.

As I have recounted above, I have also interacted with a very strange human being. He was short and odd-looking, like somebody who had stopped maturing before puberty. He was childlike, but also, when I saw him up close, oddly weathered. If you can imagine somebody who had never reached puberty but had nevertheless continued to age, that's how he appeared.

Was he, therefore, the outcome of some sort of genetic manipulation? It seems possible.

So the question remains burning, now that we know that the implants are a genuine mystery: What motive has brought our visitors here, and why are they so secretive?

CHAPTER 6
What Might They Want?

IN APRIL OF 1977, T. B. H. KUIPER OF THE JET Propulsion Lab and Mark Morris, then a research fellow at the Owens Valley Radio Observatory, published a paper in the magazine *Science*, titled "Searching for Extraterrestrial Civilizations," that contained a number of interesting speculations about how such civilizations might view us, which have been borne out by my personal experience, and which also speak to the issue of why they might choose to conceal themselves. Understand, no matter what the actual origin of this intelligence is, extraterrestrial or not, their speculations remain appropriate, because they would be true of any advanced intelligence, no matter where it came from or what it was.

The paper was published during a more free era, when credentialed scientists could speculate about extraterrestrial contact without fear of compromising their careers. It's sad that the skeptics have been so effective in shutting down this vital line of scientifically informed

69

speculation, because, even after more than thirty years, this paper remains state-of-the-art in terms of sophisticated thought about the possibility of contact. The best we have managed more recently is Stephen Hawking's rather constricted warning that extraterrestrials might turn out to be dangerous.

The authors suggest that "if the cost and speed of interstellar travel are practicable, and the probability of the evolution of intelligent life in 10/10 years is not very small, then, following the arguments in this article, there should be some explanation why we are not in open contact with extraterrestrial beings."

They go on to say that "knowledge, in a general sense, that encompasses science and culture, is likely to be most highly prized by an advanced civilization." And then comes what could be the primary reason that the intelligence that is here appears to be so interested in concealing its observation of us behind a cloud of questions: "Before a certain threshold is reached, complete contact with a superior civilization (in which most of their knowledge is made available to us) would abort further development through a 'culture shock' effect." They continue that, if we were contacted too early, the best human minds might be absorbed for generations in digesting the technology and culture of the more advanced civilization, and "by intervening in our natural progress now, members of an extraterrestrial society could easily extinguish the only resource on this planet that could be of any value to them."

On a few occasions, I had the chance to ask a question of a visitor. For the most part, this happened deep in the woods at night. If I glimpsed one of them, I would sit on the ground and collect myself, enter a meditative state, and then ask my question aloud.

Usually, there was no response—in general, I suppose, because they weren't really there. But on some occasions, they were, and once when I asked a question I got a response that I feel was supportive of Kuiper and Morris's speculation. I asked, "What does the universe mean to you?"

Instantly, there appeared in my mind a bright, clear image of a closed coffin.

I cannot explain how this was done, but can only say that these vivid, television-like images were a common way they had of communicating with me. I might add that they were also among the strangest things I have ever known. They weren't simple images. With them came what I can only describe as a sense of person, an intimacy of being, that conveyed a taste of the personality that had created them.

Had I been more practiced at this, I think that I would have found that a whole personal history was being conveyed with such an image. Even now, looking back on that moment, I can taste of that being in his loneliness and the beauty of his mind, and his sense of himself as commonplace, a working man walking in a forest at night, far from home.

I wondered how anybody could think of our mysterious universe this way? But then I realized that, of course, they have probably reached its limits, or worse, discovered that reality has no limits.

I can see the claustrophobia that would attend to the realization that one was trapped in an infinity that could never be escaped. In fact, I can feel it. It's a little like being in a room you can never leave, or a prison.

But if there are universes beyond this one—and the evidence is growing that there is at least one—then an even deeper sense of meaninglessness intrudes. Stephen Hawking's contention that the big bang was an inevitable outcome of the void, and was not instigated by a creator at all, comes to seem more probable. Infinity, being forever beyond comprehension, is also beyond meaning.

Beginners like us, constantly struck by the new, would offer escape, maybe the only escape to somebody who understands that they are trapped in infinity. And this is why one of the most profound aspects of close encounter may be very near the heart of their motive for hiding themselves.

In 1950 the physicist Enrico Fermi asked why, if there are advanced civilizations in our galaxy, they haven't shown up here.

The short answer is that, if they have, Fermi and his friends at Los Alamos didn't know it or wouldn't face it.

The argument, still advocated by many, is that they couldn't get here because the distances are too great.

There is no way that we know of—now. But that could change at any time. For example, in 2007 physicists at the University of Michigan demonstrated that what Albert Einstein called "spooky action at a distance" between two atoms could be brought about not by bringing the atoms into contact and then separating them but merely by entangling photons that they had emitted. As a result, prodding one of the atoms caused the other atom a meter away to react as if it was prodded too. Additionally, laser beams have been successfully teleported, or moved from one location to another, using quantum-physical principles.

Right now, these are exotic experiments. But they do imply that movement through space as we understand it is not the only way that things traverse this universe, so it's not ridiculous to assume that somebody very much in advance of us might use quite exotic means to defeat the gulf of distance that characterizes the universe.

Better to look at the evidence: it's clear that *somebody* is here—alien or not, I cannot say. But I remember those strange, insectlike faces I woke up to find staring at me in December of 1985. I also remember the people who put in the implant. And I remember others, many others, some human and some not, but all similar in one respect: they came out of the unknown and presented me with incredible questions. They transformed my life and my understanding of the world. And, lest I doubt that they were real, they left an implant in my ear. I have only to reach up and touch it, and the whole of the mystery once again washes over me.

What would the world be like without mysteries? It is a claustrophobic and desperate idea. And what if it goes on forever, endlessly repeating itself, star upon star, galaxy upon galaxy, universe upon universe?

If so, then there is truly no escape, not for anybody who understands this as a certainty. For them, it is indeed a coffin, and our innocence is a kind of freedom that must be among the most precious things that they know.

PART TWO

The Extreme Strangeness of the Evidence

L OOKED AT AS A WHOLE, THE EVIDENCE OUR VISI- tors have deposited appears like a discreet but ambi- tious excursion into a primitive world by an advanced species. Also, though, it is just incredibly strange. Fan- tastically strange.

Could it be that intelligent life, when it discovers that it is trapped in eternity, inevitably goes mad, and therefore that our visitors are, by any standard except perhaps their own, insane?

In this section, I will review in detail the different types of physi- cal evidence that have been deposited among us. This evidence is extensive and leads to some deeply shocking discoveries about the presence that is behind it. Using present knowledge and equipment, it could easily be studied scientifically.

Looked at in the aggregate, it suggests that a stealthy and many- leveled process of penetration of our world and our lives is taking place. The physical evidence says that man and man's world are being entered by something that is moving with the utmost care, but is always moving, and always coming closer. The slow relentlessness of it is reminiscent of the way predators like snakes approach their prey. Only when the snake is too close to miss does it strike.

This penetration is much more complex, of course, because there is also a level of it that seems to be about acclimatization, or even involves a process that is intended to alter the way reality is perceived by the human mind.

Still, it comes down to this: are we being seen as wild animals that need to be tamed to a new and higher level of reality, with all the promise that implies, or are we prey being entered by stealthy tendrils until, in the end, we will be consumed?

Or are the two things the same?

CHAPTER 7
A Secret History

A FTER IT BECAME CLEAR TO ME, IN EARLY 1986, that what had happened to me the previous December was a real event, and not a hallucination or a nightmare, I began to research the whole field of UFOs. When I was a boy, I'd been fascinated, but one does tend to leave the things of childhood behind.

As my experiences continued, Anne and I embarked on a long journey through what turns out to be one of the most extensive and complex—and most ignored—literatures in the world: that of the unidentified flying object and the close encounter.

We were aware of the fact that what had come into our lives was a great secret, surrounded by skillfully managed lies that left the twin impressions that the whole field was nonsense and the research unimportant.

The exact opposite was the truth. The field is enormously important, and many of the researchers, operating under the most adverse possible conditions and generally with few professional skills and no funding, have accomplished an astonishing amount of credible work.

The contradiction between the fact that the visitors are real and that most people remain passive did not seem to either of us to be an accident. It couldn't be an accident. It must have been an outcome of policy.

When I was taken, it seemed to me that there was an intentional effort to awaken me. I was meant to see what I saw. I was meant to end up facing the reality of the visitors, but with only the smallest amount of evidence and almost no information. I was meant to put it together for myself.

Anne realized this early on, and we decided together to respond by embarking on a journey of research that included not only my own experiences but also the experiences of others and the research that had been done.

Modern UFO research mostly involved cases that had taken place since the 1940s. But we wondered if we couldn't learn more by going back further, perhaps to the earliest modern cases. And, in fact, some of the most revealing cases had actually unfolded in the 1930s.

The combination of theatricality and secrecy appears too carefully orchestrated to be an accident. It would seem more likely that they are an outcome of policy. They will show themselves in the skies, while at the same time concealing the intimacy of their actual involvement with us.

But how does this policy function? What sort of thinking has gone into it?

In order to see the outlines of their policy, it is necessary to observe it on as large a scale as possible. That way, it should be possible to discover consistencies that reveal their guiding principles, and therefore the thinking behind them. From that, perhaps it would be possible to begin to understand something. For the most part, the UFO literature consisted of case narratives, which were mostly devoted to advocacy in the face of denial.

Anne and I were beyond that level of question. I had been assaulted and we both knew it. My memory wasn't faulty. My brain wasn't diseased or injured. We knew that at last one case was real.

Even as my own experience proceeded and deepened, we found one good reason why our visitors might be secretive. The military— and not just the U.S. military—had been shooting at our visitors for a long time.

There was no mystery about this. If we went to another planet and got shot at, we'd be damn careful too.

The record now shows pretty conclusively that we shoot at the visitors, so whatever policy they have developed regarding us must take this into account.

A typical report comes from Ontario, California. On August 26, 2010, at approximately 9:15 p.m., witnesses claim to have observed an object in the sky at low altitude. It was triangular in shape, and they could see its metallic structure reflecting the city lights. As a second object appeared, a helicopter approached, attempting to light them up with its spotlight. The two objects then maneuvered in such a way that they seemed to be trying to gain position on each other. A moment later, bright sparks began to appear between them. They and the helicopter then flew out of sight, and soon a jet appeared in the area, followed by an even larger plane, both of which also flew out of sight.

Anecdotal descriptions like this have, of course, a limited value, but there are also well-documented accounts of military activity in relation to UFOs.

One such case took place in Iran on September 18, 1976, at about eleven at night. The event was witnessed by four airmen in two fighter aircraft, the personnel guiding them to the target in the tower, and the general and other personnel on duty that night in the air force command post. The object was tracked both on ground and on aircraft radars. It was approximately the size of a Boeing 707, but its configuration and flight characteristics in no way matched those of a large jet, or, in fact, any aircraft.

The primary report of the object was filed by Colonel (now General, ret.) Parviz Jafari.

I interviewed him for my radio program in 2005, and found him to be a very precise, accurate man who was clearly operating at a high level of professionalism.

His jet was among two scrambled to investigate a bright object being observed over Tehran by citizens. People had called the air-traffic-control tower at Mehrabad Airport, and the controller, Houssain Pirouzi, could observe the object visually from his post. It was flashing bright lights and appeared to be changing shape. It was at an altitude of six thousand feet.

So there was clearly a very intentional display taking place, and it's worth asking what might have been in the minds of whoever was creating it. First, there is no direct evidence that what was being seen was an alien spacecraft of some sort. In fact, its actual nature—let alone its origin—remains a complete unknown.

What happened next was that the traffic controller reported the presence of the unknown lights to the military and an Iranian air force jet was sent aloft from nearby Shahrokhi Air Base to investigate. It was an F-4 II piloted by Captain Aziz Khani, with navigator Hossein Shokri.

They soon sighted the object and tried to approach it, but every time they attempted to close, their instruments failed and they had to break off the contact. Colonel Jafari then took off with his navigator, First Lieutenant Jalal Damirian. They observed a brilliantly multi-colored object, diamond-shaped, moving low over the city of Tehran below them. He wrote, "It was flashing with intense red, green, orange and blue lights." They got a good radar return on the object, which was twenty-seven miles ahead of them. Jafari armed his weapons and prepared to fire at it—whereupon his weapons jammed and his radio became garbled. They had closed to within twenty-five miles when the object jumped back to a distance of twenty-seven miles in an instant—as, in fact, some sort of projection or reflection might be able to do.

However, projections and reflections cannot prevent cannons from being fired and electronic instruments from functioning.

The next thing Jafari knew, the lighted object had launched something at him—a ball of light. It closed fast. He was frightened, as it looked to him like a missile. He selected an AIM-9 heat-seeking missile to attempt to intercept it. But when he prepared to fire, his entire instrument array, including the firing mechanism, failed. He lost his radio.

The small object came close to his aircraft and stopped at the five o'clock position. The larger object approached, and the smaller one reentered it.

The encounter didn't end there, though. In a few seconds, the primary device ejected another small object, also described as "a round, bright light."

Jafari's radio was working again, and he was ordered to come back to base, but when he turned he discovered another object behind him. It appeared to him as a thin rectangle with a light at each end and one in the middle. His navigator could see a translucent dome with a dim light inside.

At that moment, yet another bright object was emitted, but this time it headed toward the ground, lighting a wide area of desert as it descended. Instead of hitting the ground, it landed. The light it was emitting was so bright that Jafari could see the desert for fifteen miles around the object. Incredibly, the object on the ground began broadcasting an emergency beacon that was picked up not only by Jafari but also by nearby airliners.

He then landed as ordered and was debriefed the next day, including by an American colonel, Olin Mooy, who commented, when he reported his attempt to attack the object, "You're lucky you couldn't fire." He didn't elaborate, and Jafari never saw him again.

In September of 2010, I asked researcher Linda Moulton Howe, who has worked with me for years, to talk with Colonel Mooy. I had hoped that he would shed some light on his comment to General Jafari, but he didn't say anything more about the case than is in the report he originally prepared about it. This report is in the public record, thanks to the efforts of UFO investigators, who obtained it under a Freedom of Information Act request. So if Colonel Mooy knows more, he's keeping it to himself.

On medical examination, it was found that neither Colonel Jafari's blood nor that of his navigator was coagulating, but there were no other ill effects, and the coagulation problem eventually disappeared.

A survey of the area where the object had come down revealed a curious effect: the emergency beacon was still broadcasting, but nothing could be found in the area.

Colonel Mooy's detailed description of the event was circulated to the Air Force, the NSA, the CIA, and the White House. Colonel Roland Evans provided an assessment for the Defense Intelligence Agency that stated that the case "meets all the criteria necessary for a valid study of the UFO phenomenon."

Nevertheless, there was no open change in U.S. policy regarding UFOs, and the debate remains unchanged to this day: one side claims that such objects are extraterrestrial craft and the other says they're nothing, and there the debate uselessly remains.

It is worth discussing what might have happened on that night, though—not in terms of whether or not an extraterrestrial visitor was present, but just why this particular sort of display might have been undertaken.

First, it is not unreasonable to infer from Colonel Mooy's remark that other confrontational incidents have had less benign outcomes. And, in fact, I knew of one as a boy.

In 1948, Captain Thomas Mantell had died while chasing a UFO over Kentucky. The Air Force had eventually announced that he had been mistakenly chasing Venus, ascended to too high an altitude, and lost consciousness due to his lack of oxygen equipment.

As it happened, Colonel Guy Hix, the commander of Godman Field, where the incident took place, was, by the mid-fifties, living a block away from my childhood home in San Antonio, and his son and I played together on occasion. I don't recall Colonel Hix talking about the incident, but his son thought that Mantell had chased a flying saucer. I believe that Colonel Hix may have been retired because of the incident, and I did have the impression that there was something mysterious about it.

Later, it was also attributed to then secret U.S. Navy balloon experiments. But the night after it happened, there were numerous UFO sightings in the area. Civilian air traffic controller Albert R. Pickering watched an object circle three times at low altitude. He described it as "a great big round red object." According to an interview he gave to UFO investigator William E. Jones, it then ascended at incredible speed, stopped as if it had hit a wall, then descended, remained close to the ground for a short time, then took off, never to be seen again.

Not a balloon, then.

But knowledge of an incident like that cannot have been the only reason that Colonel Mooy would have made the comment that he did.

In October of 2008, the British Ministry of Defense (MoD) released a large number of previously classified UFO files. Included among them was a report to the effect that two USAF pilots had been ordered to scramble to intercept a UFO on the night of May 20, 1957, from RAF Manston in Kent.

One of the pilots, Milton Torres, was still alive when the report was released, along with a letter of inquiry he had written in 1988 requesting further information about what had transpired that night. After the MoD released the report, Torres gave interviews explaining that he had been ordered to fire his entire salvo of twenty-four MK-40 rockets at the object, which, he said, "gave the radar return of an aircraft carrier." The radar blip was so intense that he thought his screen would be damaged by it.

"It was the best target" he had ever locked onto, because it was so large. But as soon as he did, the object started moving. It was also visible on the scope at Manston ground control, and Torres approached to within thirty miles of it. He could not see it visually because of cloud cover. Then it disappeared from radar. When neither he nor ground control could pick it up again, he was ordered to return to base, which he did.

After the mission, he was informed by a representative of the National Security Agency that it was classified and he was not to speak about it. Until the story appeared in worldwide news in 2008, he held his silence, and one must wonder how many others do so to this day.

Initially, when the MoD report was released, it was claimed by U.S. officials that the radar blip was an electronic anomaly created under a CIA program called Palladium, which used advanced radar equipment to generate false returns. However, Palladium did not begin until the early 1960s.

In 2008, Torres told CNN, "It was some kind of space alien craft. It was so fast, it was so incredible. . . . It was absolutely death-defying."

It was also another example of an aggressive military response to a UFO. Of course, in this case, there is at least a shadow of question because of the existence of Project Palladium. It could have been an early experiment with generating a false radar return, before Palladium was formally initiated.

However, that is not true of the Iranian case, or of a 1980 Peruvian case where a pilot actually fired on a UFO without result but then was able to fly to within a few hundred feet of it and observe a craft with a dome, dimly lit from inside.

There are many such cases, and undoubtedly many more that remain as classified, as the Torres case was before the MoD released it.

What appears from the available record is that military aircraft often respond aggressively to UFOs, but generally are not, in turn, attacked. So either Colonel Mooy had information that remains classified or he was speculating.

In any case, each of these incidents reveals two things: first, a display of what I would describe as "might," and second, one of defensive capability.

If we were attempting to acclimatize a frightened and aggressive, but less advanced, species on another planet, this is one way we might approach the matter. We would want to appear to them to be too powerful to attack, and also to show them that our own intentions were not aggressive.

But we would also do the same thing if we wanted to intimidate them into both keeping our presence secret and leaving us free to act in their world without interference from them.

So it cannot be said that the lack of aggressive response is an indication of a benevolent intention. It may be precisely the opposite, and the clever part of it is that by not responding aggressively, our visitors have put us in a position of being unable to determine what their motives are, benevolent or exploitative, or if they are something more like guards, who will remain passive to us unless we attempt to leave earth, much as the keepers on a great African game preserve will leave the animals alone unless they move off-range.

But how can we tell? Is there any way to advance the question beyond this faintly disturbing speculation?

What we can most usefully do, I think, is to go back to the time when the modern phenomenon began to emerge, before anybody had shot at anybody, before we had any idea even about the possibility of aliens, before the words "flying disk" had ever been uttered.

CHAPTER 8
A Real Mirage

IN 2010, A BOOK CALLED *MIRAGE MEN* WAS PUB-
lished claiming that UFO reports were a cover designed
by the U.S. Air Force to create confusion around the
testing of secret aircraft during the cold war. However,
UFO sightings were professionally documented before the cold war
and, in fact, before the U.S. Air Force existed, or any American air
force beyond a few biplanes.

It is popularly believed that the first modern UFO incidents took
place in the mid- to late 1940s, but Anne and I found that the modern process of mysterious sightings, reports, and involvement of the
authorities began in the 1930s. Prior to 1931, there had been scattered
reports going back into the historical past, but the particular structure
of observation of disks or lights, witness reports, media coverage, and
official investigation started that year.

In the 1890s, there had been a series of mysterious airship sightings
starting in the west and spreading into the eastern United States, finally

ending in 1896. If the whole thing wasn't a hoax perpetrated by news-paper reporters, then these sightings certainly involved a high level of strangeness. One airship came to rest just inches from some sur-prised citizens, then disappeared, to be replaced by a man, who calmly explained that he had a device that enabled him to compress it to the point that it could fit in his pocket! These playful stories also involved vehicles piloted by beautiful nude women, as well as a considerable amount of "editing" by local newspapermen. Nevertheless, at one point the stories were so numerous that Thomas Edison was compelled to issue a statement that the airships did not belong to him.

Many of the reports suggested that the occupants were from Mars, and in modern times one of the only consistent indicators of UFO waves has been Mars oppositions. When Mars is closest to earth, UFO sightings rise—either because the planet is so prominent that it causes people to make mistakes or perhaps because the Martians are a frugal race, and don't want to spend any more energy than they must in order to get here.

But, of course, the reality is that the consistent connection between UFO waves and Mars oppositions is just another factor that must be either proved or disproved and, if true, understood.

On October 11, 1931, the first truly modern event took place at Gallipolis Ferry, West Virginia, and, as this one involved the police, it's less likely to have been a hoax. Witnesses saw what appeared to be a flaming dirigible crash. Instead of telling the local newspaper or treat-ing it as a joke, they reacted in a new way. Thinking that they had seen a disaster, they informed the authorities.

For visitors observing the effects of this demonstration, this would mean that a new level of response had emerged in the culture.

The police investigated but could find no sign of a dirigible crash, and nothing was ever reported. So perhaps it was a meteor. Meteor falls are frequently mistaken for UFO events. They can appear deceptively slow, can display flames, can look very much like a crashing aircraft.

But then, just over a year later, an event that was slightly more difficult to explain took place a few hundred miles away. On December 29, 1932, New Jersey police were informed by a witness that he had seen the lights of an aircraft descending into some trees. There was an immediate search-and-rescue operation, but nothing was found.

The lights of an aircraft descending into trees sounds a lot less like a meteor fall. In fact, it sounds a good deal like many modern nighttime UFO sightings. In this sense, it is just a bit less ambiguous than the 1931 sighting.

These two events marked the first time that there had been an officially organized response to a strange sighting of this type. It is almost as if the first was an experiment designed to see if social structures robust enough to carry out such an investigation had evolved. So a second experiment, somewhat more enigmatic, was tried nearby, and the result was observed. This time, the apparent crash resulted in a more elaborate response.

This may have meant to our visitors that a new phase in the relationship could begin. The criteria seem to have been very specific: to present humanity with questions that could neither be ignored nor answered. And this, I think, is the consistent core of the entire human experience of the visitors, and, as I will discuss, is the engine of the change in our brains and our minds that they are causing.

In the 1930s, only a few people were faced by such questions. By the time another quarter century had passed, many millions of people were wondering about the mysterious flying saucers. Now the mystery is part of our common culture, rejected only by our elites, who have a stake in continuing the illusion that they control human affairs. But they do not control human affairs. The visitors do.

Because they do not want to face this, UFO studies are the last real taboo of the cultural elites, and witnesses are the last social class that can be lampooned with impunity and discriminated against without compunction. Two hundred years ago, punters could pay a few pence to tour Bedlam and laugh at the insane. The same people who would never think now of doing something so barbarous will willingly deride and ostracize a close-encounter witness, and think it their obligation to ignore somebody like me, lest giving attention to the questions that I raise contaminate the culture.

In the summer of 1932, our visitors may have attempted another experiment. This was a neat escalation from the falling lights of winter, in that it was the first encounter with the organized aggressive elements in human society, in the form, in this case, of the British RAF.

On July 5, 1932, over Sussex, not far from where Milton Torres would have his encounter twenty-five years later, four Royal Air Force Hawker Fury I biplanes reported that a gigantic light was shining down from above into the center of their formation. Two of the planes immediately began to have mechanical trouble, and left the formation. One of the pilots, who passed through the light on the way down, experienced burns on his face and hands. These are reminiscent of the burns experienced by Betty Cash and Vickie and Colby Landrum on December 29, 1980, when they encountered a diamond-shaped UFO emitting flames on an isolated road in east Texas. They counted twenty-three helicopters surrounding this object, but in a subsequent attempt to sue the U.S. government over the injuries they received, they were unable to prove their origin and so lost the suit.

Betty Cash, who was the worst burned in the incident, died on its nineteenth anniversary. She never recovered her health, but there is no record of what happened to the young RAF pilot who was burned.

Over the autumn of 1932, mysterious aircraft were seen over England and the U.S. east coast, and then in December of 1933, there was another escalation, when unusual planes began to be reported over Sweden. This was the first "UFO flap," and was strikingly similar to one that took place over Belgium in 1989 and 1990.

A mysterious airplane was operating in northern Norway and Sweden, but the Swedish air force was unable to find it. It could fly in weather that grounded the planes of the era, and was often seen flying very low, shining a powerful searchlight on the ground. In Belgium, the objects were triangular or rectangular in shape, but they also shone incredibly bright lights down to the ground.

At one point during the Swedish flap, it was believed that the planes were flying out of an airfield hidden in the mountains. When airborne reconnaissance failed, a young officer set out on skis. He never returned. A rescue squad followed him. They, also, never returned.

As would become the case worldwide, the mysterious craft concentrated on military installations, almost as if they were trying to provoke a reaction—which, of course, they probably were.

Were we to be in the position of observing a less advanced species on another world, we might also be able to learn a great deal from exposing ourselves to them in this way. Certainly, though, if they had a lot in common with us, we might do things quite differently. And, in fact, judging from the slowness with which our own visitors are proceeding, and the extent of their intervention into, for example, our sexual content, it might be worth assuming until shown to be otherwise that they find us extremely strange, and are quite possibly struggling in an effort to understand us well enough to establish common ground.

Phantom plane sightings continued across Sweden, Norway, and Finland through 1935. Generally, they appeared as large gray aircraft, sometimes seen in formations of three. They often flew in impossible weather conditions. Mysterious radio signals were also picked up, and one newspaper attempted an exploratory investigation but was prevented by the Norwegian military from entering the area where the planes seemed to be coming from.

It was assumed that the planes must be Soviet or German reconnaissance aircraft, but it has subsequently become clear that no country in the world possessed planes at that time that could do things like fly at night in snowstorms.

Shipping in mid-Atlantic reported mystery planes at a time when transatlantic flights were still rare, but nobody capable of executing them claimed to be doing so.

In 1937, even stranger objects appeared along the Polish-German border in the form of flying swords and coffins. Then, in 1938, glowing orbs began to be seen in British skies, as they still are to this day.

In the summer of that year, one of the first classic flying-saucer sightings took place in Massachusetts, when a Somerville resident observed a silent, metallic object passing overhead in the moonlight. It had four rectangular portholes that glowed with orange light. He observed the silhouettes of figures looking down at him.

The sequence of sightings had moved from observations of apparently conventional aircraft to a near flyby of a more streamlined object containing recognizable silhouettes.

Prior to the age of flight, objects like orbs or disks were seen on occasion, but as soon as human flight began, the mystery objects began to parallel known designs. This continued until the 1938 Massachusetts sighting, which was the first recorded instance of a flying disk in modern times, and the first involving figures since the mystery airships of the 1890s.

So far, there was not the slightest suggestion or idea that these might be extraterrestrial spacecraft, or that their occupants might be anything other than what they seemed—human beings.

There is a coherent structure to this sequence of sightings that suggests not an attempt at direct contact but something more in the nature of a process of probing human culture with an eye to eliciting reactions that could be studied and observed.

It is consistent with an approach by an extraterrestrial species, certainly, but, as I have said, there are very deep waters running here, and there is every reason to continue to adhere to the question and not answer it by concluding that aliens have arrived. By doing so, we will draw some quite amazing facts to the surface, because if we are experiencing an interaction with aliens from another planet, then, as I will discuss, there are things that they are doing that are stranger than it is almost possible to imagine. However, another even more extraordinary reality will emerge in the context of exploring this question: so are we.

CHAPTER 9

The Single Most Important UFO Case

ANNE AND I WERE OFTEN TOLD BY MEM-
bers of the skeptical community that there
were no really well-developed cases of professional observers witnessing unidentified
flying objects that were not eventually identified. We found out that
the opposite was true. In fact, there are many such cases, and one that
stands out as one of the most compelling of all UFO cases.

Dr. Paul Hill is exceptional as a UFO witness not only because
of his experience and stature but also for his practical engineering
expertise and the extraordinary UFO sightings that he had. They
included other witnesses, both professional and nonprofessional, and
he recorded in detail the flight characteristics of the objects he saw.

Dr. Hill began his illustrious career as an engineer at NACA, the
predecessor of NASA, and was a recipient of NASA's highest award
for scientific achievement, the Distinguished Service Award, after a
lifetime of engineering achievement. His credentials as an aeronautical

engineer are above reproach. He also wrote one of the very best and most important books on the subject of UFOs, *Unconventional Flying Objects*.

In July of 1952, this prominent engineer had one of the most spectacular UFO sightings of all time. When it happened, he was working on flying platform technology, and by experiment soon determined that his craft could duplicate the flight characteristics of what he had observed, albeit with far less power. So he concluded that the UFO operated a very efficient static field technology—in effect, pushing against the ground to maintain lift, just like his platform. He was even able to duplicate the familiar "falling leaf" motion of the UFO on his flying platform.

It may be surprising to know what he accomplished. Although he should be an important historical figure, few people have ever heard of him. For example, the prominent members of the skeptical community, who I initially assumed would have the answers, never even mentioned his existence.

The relentless rejection of the UFO phenomenon makes us, as a society, forgetful of what has been learned in the past. It's as if every few years the whole debate starts anew.

In fact, though, it has a long history, including a history of professional-level observations of the very highest quality.

Dr. Hill made careful estimates of altitude and speed of craft he observed, and was privy to a 1952 case that involved multiple radar measurement of speed with visual confirmation by professional observers.

It is distressing that the scientific community did not pick up on cases like this, and no mainstream foundation ever granted in the field, and no scientific institution ever took up the study.

NASA played an important role in this intellectual and cultural tragedy, in that it suppressed Dr. Hill's work until after his death, meaning that he could not be an effective advocate during his lifetime.

One result of NASA's failure is probably that we are still traveling in jets and using rockets, as we have never followed up on Dr. Hill's observations on UFO propulsion and the means that must be in use to accomplish it. It could be that because NASA refused to address the matter methodically and productively as soon as it became apparent that UFOs were real objects, we have remained essentially a trapped species, and are now facing dieback or even extinction as our planet becomes unable to support us. To gain the secret of UFO propulsion, we probably have years of work yet to do. That work should have started a generation ago.

Dr. Hill's 1952 sighting was part of a massive UFO incursion that took place over the summer of that year. This huge flap involved sensational sightings over Washington, and the Air Force's attempt to explain them as temperature inversions was not convincing to many people.

Apparently they weren't convincing to official Washington, either, because after the 1952 flap, reports from military personnel detailing the speed and performance of unknown flying objects were classified by Joint Army, Navy, Air Force Publication 146 and Air Force Regulation 200-2, and this classification has never been lifted. So the military is under a legal obligation to lie when it is asked about its UFO policy. It must respond that it has no data and does not concern itself with the matter.

The media chooses to take what is demonstrably a lie as real, actual fact. I say "demonstrably" because Air Force reports from prior to the classification order remain on the record. The media is under no legal obligation to cooperate with the official world in suppressing UFO information. It's a choice that has become a part of the institution, largely because it was made in support of the military years ago, and probably requested by the military, at a time when it was normal and acceptable for media outlets to agree uncritically to such requests. But that time has passed. At present, there is only one professional investigative reporter working in this field, Leslie Kean. Given the truly incredible scoop that could come from energetic reporting, it's surprising that there aren't more. But such is the prejudice that has built up over the years against the topic that, as Ms. Kean has told me, most established media outlets—in particular, major newspapers—will not allow their staff to cover the subject at all.

Thus no media coverage and no scientific investigation. But that does not need to remain the case, because there are now elements in the private sector, such as Space X and Bigelow Aerospace, among others, that could take up this study with the hope of eventually resolving issues such as UFO propulsion.

We can observe UFOs in flight. We have a substantial worldwide archive at this point of usable data, and this can be used to make the beginning that should have been made all that time ago.

Back before the military classified its observations, they were commonly reported and often in detail, and Major Donald E. Keyhoe's *Flying Saucers from Outer Space* and Major Edward Ruppelt's *The Report on Unidentified Flying Objects* both contain detailed accounts from professional observers that include radar observations, accurate speed and altitude data, and carefully observed flight characteristics.

Pilots still see these objects all the time. Social opprobrium and airline policy, however, generally prevent all but the most sketchy reports.

Airlines must shift from suppressing such reports and penalizing pilots for making them, to encouraging them. In addition, there needs to be a data-collection facility that has a high level of capability but operates entirely outside of any official context. Pilot reports submitted to the Federal Aviation Administration, for example, will come under the purview of security regulations and, if they involve objects of unknown origin, they may be transmitted to the military and disappear into the classification system, where, in all probability, they will be filed away and forgotten.

The FAA has announced that it will give all such reports to Bigelow Aerospace, but unless the reports involve known objects that are believed by the military to be harmless, they are liable to classification. So what will the FAA actually transmit—sketchy, civilian accounts or detailed pilot and traffic-control reports backed up by radar tracks? One guess would be that nothing but anecdotal reports without any detail will be what is provided to Bigelow Aerospace.

But things like radar tracks do exist, and not only from the past but also from recent UFO events. In January 2008, there were a substantial number of UFO sightings in and around Stephenville, Texas, that attracted the interest of the Mutual UFO Network (MUFON), a loose affiliation of interested parties that has developed investigative protocols that enable amateur investigators to generate field reports of good quality.

Subsequent to discovering that military aircraft had been seen in the area in conjunction with the UFO sightings, MUFON investigators instituted a total of ten Freedom of Information Act requests, which resulted in the FAA providing 2.8 million radar returns for the night of January 8 to 9, 2008. Working with this data and a redacted fighter squadron logbook provided by nearby Carswell Air Force Base under a Freedom of Information Act request, the investigators were able to identify a total of ten sorties from the base on that night, and there are likely to be more under the redactions.

At first, the early sorties remained in a military training area, but then they suddenly turned on transponders and departed from that area, moving to the Stephenville area at the same time that the public UFO observations were taking place. An aircraft was also tracked on FAA radar flying a "racetrack" course at forty-one thousand feet, characteristic of an AWACS electronic control system on station. What's more, FAA radar reveals an unknown target in the area that the fighters entered.

Obviously, a military exercise took place, but the AWACS remained in the area for four hours, long after the fighters had left and the unknown object had disappeared.

It is not unreasonable to assume that there was some reason that the fighters moved into the area where the unknown object was located. Certainly, from the ground, this is what witnesses who saw them seemingly give chase to the unknown craft concluded.

So radar tracks exist. Not only that, it's likely that civilian airliners detect UFOs on their radars, but the pilots never report them, for the reasons discussed above.

One would hope that operations such as this, concealed behind the wall of classification, are based on knowledge and lead to knowledge.

Never imagine, though, that classification hides professionalism. Far from it, the rampant secrecy of the U.S. government, when it is broken, as often as not turns out to be concealing waste, indifferent research, poor record-keeping, and inferior thinking. The reason for the latter is simple enough: scientists of real talent want to publish in the peer-reviewed press. I know scientists who work in sensitive areas who live in fear that their research will be classified and their ability to advance in their professions compromised. Official secrecy is a dead hand and a smotherer of innovation, so it can hardly be expected that much useful advance has been made in secret facilities, especially when it comes to a phenomenon as esoteric as unidentified flying objects, and the immensely subtle and complex intelligence that lies behind them.

There is no reason to assume that research done behind closed doors is especially qualified, and every reason to assume that it is not. So until proven otherwise by full disclosure of records that suggest that at least a somewhat intellectually sophisticated approach has been taken, it's probably safe to think that the mere process of classifying in this area has impeded progress at virtually every level, and resulted in conclusions of indifferent quality at best.

On the night of July 14, 1952, two Pan American Airlines pilots,

William B. Nash and William H. Fortenberry, flying on a route over the Chesapeake Bay, reported seeing six flying objects moving in formation between their aircraft and the ground. Both were not only experienced pilots, they had flown in World War II and were trained in procedures for in-flight identification of aircraft. Their observation was very well executed by both men operating to high professional standards, and their reporting of it was meticulous. It was listed as a genuine unknown by the Project Blue Book investigation that was carried out under the management of Dr. Edward Condon of the University of Colorado UFO Project in the 1960s.

Project Blue Book has been criticized for concluding that there was no reason to continue official UFO investigations, while at the same time indicating that a number of provocative cases were genuine unknowns. When I spoke at the University of Colorado's Conference of World Affairs in 1988, I was introduced by Dr. Walter Orr Roberts, the founder of the National Center for Atmospheric Research, who told me in conversation that he had been asked to chair what became known as the Condon Committee, the group that managed Project Blue Book. He said that he was told frankly by Air Force personnel that the purpose of the committee was to issue a finding that UFO studies were "worthless." He said, "They told me they wanted to get out of the UFO business."

Of course they did. Given that their own personnel could not legally disseminate UFO reports or information, how could they possibly remain as a public investigatory resource? Since 1952, the U.S. Air Force has been leading a double life: secretly investigating UFO reports while publicly taking the position that they are not worth investigating. If they don't investigate these cases, then what was Colonel Mooy doing in Iran interviewing General Jafari? And if they're indifferent, why did Carswell's fighters enter the airspace over Stephenville that was occupied by an unknown object? And if they are not required to lie, why did Carswell officials initially deny that they had done this?

Dr. Roberts declined to chair the Project Blue Book committee, as its findings were to be a foregone conclusion. Dr. Condon was less demanding.

Project Blue Book's own records indicate that unknown objects that are all but certainly under intelligent control appear in our skies. So the abandonment of this research is not based on data. It is based on something else—which, incidentally, beyond the classification, is a much, much larger and more complicated issue. The deeper reason that the Air Force wanted to "get out of the UFO business" was probably that it can't fulfill its responsibility to protect us from airborne incursions, so it has hidden the whole matter in the vast sepulchre of official secrecy. Like NASA, it's the wrong institution, with the wrong tools and the wrong responsibilities, and, above all, the wrong legal constraints.

The immeasurably rich question of the visitors should be engaging the minds not of generals but of aeronautical engineers, physicists, anthropologists, biologists, psychiatrists, neurologists, psychologists, and sociologists, and even philosophers and theologians—and perhaps especially the latter two groups.

An hour after sunset on the night of July 14, 1952, it was clear and dark over the Chesapeake Bay, when a very bright light suddenly appeared in front of the Pan Am plane being flown by Fortenberry and Nash.

Fortenberry later described the sighting: "Almost immediately we perceived that it consisted of six bright objects streaking toward us at tremendous speed, and obviously well below us. They had the fiery aspect of hot coals, but of much greater glow, perhaps twenty times more brilliant than any of the scattered ground lights over which they passed or the city lights to the right. Their shape was clearly outlined and evidently circular; the edges were well defined, not phosphorescent or fuzzy in the least, and the red-orange color was uniform over the upper surface of each craft."

Subsequently, the objects made a spectacular maneuver while passing under the plane by flipping on their edges, then back to a horizontal position. Then they sped off into the night.

Fortunately, the sighting took place before airline pilots risked damage to their careers for reporting UFO observations, and before the press was ignoring them. Nobody explained it away as swamp gas or a flock of buzzards.

Even so, the report was not enough to advance the debate or engage serious scientific interest.

When it appeared in the papers, though, one scientist was intrigued. Dr. Hill was immediately aware that the speed and flight characteristics the pilots had observed were far beyond those of any known aircraft, and their professional expertise suggested to him that their report was accurate. Not only that, there were numerous other UFO sightings in the area, and it happened to be close to Langley, where Dr. Hill was living.

So on the evening of July 16, he and his wife drove down to the Chesapeake Bay to see if they could observe anything unusual. At eight o'clock, they saw two amber lights come toward them from the southeast. The lights passed directly over them, then slowed down and turned, soon streaking away.

Hill estimated their speed at five hundred miles an hour, and was later able to triangulate their altitude based on another sighting that was reported, this one from an aircraft spotter who was in the area. They were determined to have been at an altitude of approximately eighteen thousand feet, and to have been twenty to thirty feet in diameter.

Dr. Hill describes the sighting in his book: "They practically came to a stop as they approached. It was then that they started their strange jitter, a surprising phenomenon. First one leaped a little way ahead of the other as fast as or faster than the eye could follow. Then the other seemed to jump ahead. They kept up these odd mincing steps for a few seconds as they passed overhead. Then, after passing zenith, they made an astounding maneuver. Maintaining their spacing of about 200 feet, they revolved in a horizontal circle about a common center, at a rate of at least once per second. After a few revolutions, and without pause, they switched their revolutions into a vertical plane, keeping up the same amazing rate."

If we were attempting contact with a less-advanced species, confused about us and suspicious of us but able to understand at least some of the principles of flight and propulsion that we had mastered, we might well seek to display ourselves to one of their leading aeronautical experts, in order to show him that we were real and possessed advanced capabilities that might interest him.

So it probably isn't a coincidence that sightings took place not far from Langley, where Dr. Hill and his colleagues were likely to hear about them.

If this is what happened, then a degree of understanding of our society is certainly implied. Perhaps our visitors didn't know who Dr. Hill was, but it is conceivable that they knew that our most advanced aeronautical research was taking place at Langley, and, as would become apparent later in the month, also that our center of government was Washington, D.C.

However, there was something missing in the interaction with Dr. Hill. They offered a spectacular display, but there was, strikingly, no communication, and no attempt at any, at least none that he was able to notice.

So near and yet so far. Later in the month, Dr. Hill's sighting would be superseded by one of history's most spectacular UFO events, when dozens of objects, over a series of days, appeared above Washington, D.C. This was part of the most complex incursion in history, which showed both the skill and the ineptitude of our visitors. Or if not ineptitude, then an intentional attempt to make it seem as if communication was impossible.

In fact, though, the reasons for this lack of communication are likely to go beyond, say, linguistic issues. Also, there seems to be a contradiction involved. Why tantalize Dr. Hill, then do things that ensure that the government will begin to deny that you even exist?

If Drs. Kuiper and Morris are correct in their analysis, then our visitors' actions make sense. They would not want the government to state that they were real, because this would redirect the society toward them in exactly the way that they would want to avoid. But they *would* want to get people like Dr. Hill thinking and acting, because they would want us to develop the technologies we need to become interstellar travelers, but to do it on our own.

So when we see a combination of actions that induces official secrecy but also excites the curiosity of scientists, what we may be seeing is the enactment of policy. This policy would be to try to induce us to make the necessary discoveries ourselves, so that we don't meet them as supplicants.

This tells us two things. First, although they may well be exploiting us in many ways, there is also an underlying strata of ethical behavior that will one day be of use to us in our dealings with them. Second, they have reason to believe that we can understand enough to do the science necessary to solve the UFO propulsion problem, so they most likely consider us intellectually competent.

Going to the next step, which is communication with our visitors, will involve the greatest leap of scientific innovation and social consciousness ever undertaken by mankind. We will truly be looking at and living in a new world, if we manage it.

After his sighting, Dr. Hill was on fire with interest in flying disks. He had seen what he felt certain were intelligently guided craft. He wanted to do more about this. He wanted to learn more.

However, when he reported what he had seen to a superior at NACA, he was accused of drinking. And there, in that moment, was distilled what has become the most important human failure of all time, the inability to face this reality. Here this supervisor had one of his most distinguished and capable experts sitting before him, describing a sighting of an intelligently guided object far in advance of anything we had, and the only response he could manage was to accuse him of alcohol abuse.

This is human nature at its weakest, but it proved to be very much at the core of NASA's long-term reaction to Dr. Hill, and continues to fundamentally define the failure of the whole of human society's response to the question of our visitors. Dr. Hill's superiors refused to allow him to make any public statement about his sighting. In his book, he commented that "I was destined to remain as unidentified as the flying objects."

It went further than that. NASA refused to allow him to publish his book. In it, he offers the opinion that he will publish it after his retirement. But even that was not allowed. Dr. Hill's book was not published during his lifetime.

After his death, his daughter arranged to have this most important of all UFO books published—ironically, by Hampton Roads Press, a publisher located in the town where he'd had his first sightings. Were it not for Dr. Hill's daughter, NASA would have succeeded in completely suppressing this important document, and we would still be that much further from the advance that is so essential to our future.

One has to ask, How much has NASA succeeded in destroying? Or, for that matter, the Air Force or the Navy, or any of the many governmental entities that must have had involvement? Are there other testaments out there even more provocative than Dr. Hill's that NASA or some other agency has succeeded in strangling?

We may never know.

Nevertheless, from a scientific standpoint, Dr. Hill's book and ideas remain extremely important.

In 1960, Dr. Hill was able to make another UFO observation, thus becoming the most informed known aeronautical professional. I think that this happened because he had taken an interest in them back in 1952. I base this on my own experience. When I reacted to my December 1985 close encounter by attempting to reengage with them, they responded in two ways. First, they came back into my life. Second, they never again treated me like a lab animal. Instead, I became something like a student. I am still an eager student.

The moment that Dr. Hill made the decision to go down to the Chesapeake Bay to look for them, he almost certainly entered the visitors' awareness. Most human beings are passive. They grow to maturity, become rich or poor or both, then die. People like Dr. Hill are different. They're active. They seek knowledge and crave the new. They want more for themselves and for mankind.

If we were attempting to build a relationship with a less-advanced species, we would be extremely interested in active personalities and would do things to attract their interest, such as displaying our hardware before informed professionals like airline pilots and aerodynamic engineers. But we would also try to communicate, and the question of why our visitors have done so little of that is an important one.

The gulf that Drs. Kuiper and Morris suggested must exist, and which the actions of our visitors seem to confirm, involves at its core, I think, differences in the way we perceive and understand the world. In fact, the gulf between us and our visitors might be even greater than Kuiper and Morris speculated.

While Dr. Hill appears never to have been approached except with displays of technology, others have experienced very different sorts of approaches, including me, and as we proceed, I will detail the differences in the ways that we and our visitors see the world, insofar as I have observed, and, I hope, understood, them.

If I am correct in my analysis, then something is missing from the way we see reality—in fact, the essential thing is missing, and until we have connected with it, we will remain deaf, mute, and blind to most of the real world, and almost all of the world our visitors inhabit. They can try to get us to realize that we are blind, but they cannot open our eyes for us. That we must do ourselves.

CHAPTER 10
Crop Formations

O N THE AFTERNOON OF JULY 7, 1996, A complex, beautifully structured formation appeared in crop in a field opposite Stonehenge, just off the A303 highway, which was crowded with traffic. At 5:30 p.m., a plane had flown over the field, and it was empty. At 6:15, the formation was present. Within that forty-five-minute window, in broad daylight, it had been created without a single person seeing who had done it.

Not only that, in mathematical terms, it was a complex dynamic, and became known as the Julia Set crop formation. The thing was colossal—920 feet long and 500 feet wide, made up of 149 circles swirled into the wheat.

There were hundreds of people at Stonehenge just a few hundred yards away. On the A303 it was stop-and-start traffic. A guard at Stonehenge, glancing toward the field twice in fifteen minutes, first did not see it, then did. So it appeared inside a fifteen-minute time frame. At no time were any people seen in the field.

Now, one would think that such an amazing event would get a great deal of press attention, but what little it received was mostly laughter.

But why would this be? How could it be?

The answer is simple: the media had already decided who made the formations. It was two men, Douglas Bower and David Chorley, who had solved the riddle. They claimed in 1991 that they had created the formations by walking around at night in wheat fields with boards on their feet. Never mind that they couldn't even begin to duplicate the simplest ones. The crop they walked on for the media was visibly crushed, its stems broken, not swirled down with the stems left intact, as is true of the genuinely mysterious formations.

Nevertheless, I watched and listened in horror as the story of Doug and Dave was picked up with amazing alacrity and broadcast across the planet as if it was absolutely and finally true.

At that time, I had reason to hope that there would be an expansion in the visitors' activity on earth. Already, in 1989 and 1990, there had been a protracted UFO wave in Belgium that had been monitored in detail by the military and extensively documented at every level, from photography to witness accounts to radar. Starting in 1990, there had also been a dramatic increase in the number and complexity of the crop formations appearing in southern England, with seven hundred appearing in that year alone.

The Belgian UFO wave had been largely ignored by the general media in the English-speaking world, and had attracted no scientific interest at all. The crop formations were easier to see, though, and harder to dismiss. I was aware, before the Doug and Dave announcement, that one scientific institution was planning a large-scale study of the formations, including analysis of the soils, the condition of the crops that had been swirled down, and a number of other parameters.

Doug and Dave ended that. Nobody dared come forward, for fear that they would be greeted by gales of laughter and run out of their careers.

Once again, with one or two exceptions, such as a very determined biophysicist called William C. Levengood, there was no scientific study to speak of, and little that entered the peer-reviewed press.

To this day, far too many people, if asked, will tell you that the formations are laid down by pranksters with boards strapped to their feet.

This cannot be the case, however. Having walked in some of the formations myself, I could see perfectly clearly how the wheat had been somehow swirled down, and very little of it broken.

In the summer of 2010, Anne and I visited Wiltshire, attending the Summer Lectures at Devizes as speakers. We had occasion to walk through six or seven formations and to talk with many local people about them.

I was assured by one researcher that they were indeed all man-made, but that even the artists making them weren't quite sure how they were doing it. On the face of it, this might sound absurd, but I don't know that it is. He told us that as they pressed the crop, it would literally drop before them as if by magic, and they would even hear the plant stem nodes popping as they mysteriously bent in obedience to the artists' wishes.

While this explanation struck me as even more fanciful than the notion that aliens are doing it, I won't dismiss anything until something is proven. What sort of artistic skill set and tools might be needed to create one of the more intricate formations is hard to understand.

Much research, most of it on the part of Dr. Levengood, has shown that the stem nodes are heated to make them bend, and this is perfectly obvious even on casual observation. The nodes are darker and bent in flattened crop, but not in standing crop immediately beside it. But when I tried to bend standing crop, the stems broke off. Pushing at them with a board simply made more break than if I had done it by hand.

Not only that, I saw crop that had been intricately woven together into small, basketlike shapes. How? I tried to manipulate the wheat, which was dry and brittle, and couldn't even come close to a weaving this intricate.

The formations might be explainable—in fact, in some way, they must be. Whatever is creating them, it isn't magic. There is skill and craft behind them. They display the forms that they do for a reason. They are overwhelmingly concentrated in southern England due to factors that can, in the end, be understood.

I cannot speculate about how the formations are made, but I do think that it's reasonable to try and consider what sort of mind might be creating them, and the kind of worldview that might lie behind things like the decision to site the vast majority of them in a small area of the south of England. Of course, if the artists have all been Wiltshire pub crawlers, it would make a certain sense, but formations have been found far beyond Wiltshire, so the pub-crawling geniuses would need to be well supplied with cash for travel too.

In the summer of 1978, a farmer called Ian Stevens came across a group of five circles of crushed wheat while mowing a farm in Headbourne Worthy, and took some photographs of them, which are among the first modern crop formation images. For the most part, for the next ten years, the formations remained crude, only very slowly growing in number and in complexity.

By 1988, they had reached a greater level of sophistication and were becoming more numerous. They had also been noticed, and people were beginning to move out across Wiltshire looking for them, congregating in a pub in Devizes called the Barge Inn.

I was told in 2010 that groups of circle makers gather at the Barge Inn at night, by a woman who had worked there as a barmaid, and when we walked by late, I did see a man who seemed to be spotting outside the pub, watching for strangers. When I went closer, his cell phone appeared in his hand.

I also noticed a material difference in the formations we visited. Some of them, while beautifully designed, also seemed to contain a preponderance of broken stems and not so many heat-blown stem nodes, or no blown stem nodes. Others were intricately swirled as if by some natural force, and contained startling details, such as carefully woven designs, wheat stems that had been bunched together in spirals, and so forth.

Uniformly, they were all playful, intricate, joyous, and just simply beautiful, and I think that they were made in part by people and in part by something else, and that we might even consider them the first attempt at conversation between human beings and the unknown intelligence that is manifesting among us in so many remarkable ways.

One cannot be sure of anything in this wonderfully strange adventure, but judging from the fact that the formations have become more intricate over time, I don't know that one can conclude that this conversation was started by our visitors. It could easily have been started by people—in fact, by pranksters like Doug and Dave. The first formations were simple enough to have been created by men with boards. Even lurching drunks could have done it—if you discount the fact that even in the earliest formations, the method by which the stems were laid down involved bursts of heat that affected the nodes, causing the stems to bend. But perhaps Doug and Dave used curling irons or hair dryers.

The evolution of the formations reveals something about their creators. From the first, they have been using a technology or technique of some kind that is unknown to us, but initially they were either unable or unwilling to make elaborate formations.

Was this because they were learning how to use their equipment? Or was it because they did not want to close the question in our minds about what was happening?

If the Julia Set had been the first formation, it would have created an international sensation. People would not have been so easily convinced that it had been done by a couple of drunks, or even a pretty big crowd of them. The question might have been closed in favor of the existence of a definite mystery.

But what is being done to us is not, it seems to me, about closing questions for us. It is about opening them, and placing us in the position of being unable to answer them without careful analysis.

Not until 1993 does one begin to see formations that are really intricate, and still there is an element of crudity to them that is very markedly different from what one observes now. Whomever was making them was involved in a learning process, which certainly does suggest a human agency.

And yet, how can one explain the appearance of the Julia Set in this way? It seems disingenuous to call it a human construction, and yet leaving even this question open does keep us firmly involved in the most productive relationship to the phenomenon that we can have, which is to indulge the mystery as long as we can.

In my life, I have met some people with deep occult knowledge. Among other things, knowledge of attention. I have known people who were able to seemingly disappear before one's eyes. How did they do it? By being aware that attention is not continuous but a wave form, and not only that, when groups of people come together, their attention soon becomes entrained. If you know how, you can watch groups of people, even whole stadiums full of people, wax and wane together.

One person I knew who could do this was a longtime member of the Gurdjieff Foundation, Joseph C. Stein. I was once standing in a crowd of people, watching him come toward us down a path. The next moment, he walked up behind us.

When I asked him how he'd done it, he growled, "You figure it out." I did, and have at times been able to do it a bit myself. It's nothing supernatural, but somebody who had perfected the technique might be able to spend ten or fifteen minutes doing something like making the Julia Set and not be noticed by a single person nearby. I have to say, though, that their skill at crop formation construction would have had to be fabulous, because this immense, detailed, and perfectly measured formation was a true masterpiece. Even a team of skilled artists would have required hours to make it, if they could make it at all.

No, I don't think that the Julia Set was a word uttered by those on our side of the conversation. It was part of the music of the mystery, which seems designed as much to challenge as to delight.

By 1997, mathematical statements were appearing in the formations in the form of Koch fractals. We are expected to believe that Doug and Dave were pub-crawling about with their boards, laying down these sophisticated figures with all the mathematical knowledge and geometrical skill needed, because it was the next year that the media dismissed the whole phenomenon as their work and everybody had a good, comfortable laugh.

There is every reason to laugh with delight when contemplating the crop formations, but only a fool would allow himself to be comfortable. Nothing about the vast communication that is being sounded in our world should be taken as comfortable, because it is not comfortable. It heralds change that is going to challenge the human mind and, in the end, even our very existence—which we all sense perfectly clearly, or we wouldn't be so eager to dismiss it with childish fantasies like Doug and Dave, or the other silly explanations that are held as gospel among too many people.

Doug and Dave and their ilk didn't make the Koch fractals or the Julia Set or any of the awesome formations that have followed, as these amazing artists have found their measure, and began singing a more and more intricate and exciting song in the fields.

A good example of the level of accomplishment of the human artists could be seen in the East Field near Alton Barnes in the summer of 1998, when Mitsubishi commissioned a formation there in the shape of one of their cars. It's a well-constructed formation, somewhat

clumsy in its measurements, but nothing approaching the shocking elegance of the more mysterious formations that appeared that
summer.

Then came the explosive year of 1999, the year after Doug and
Dave were taken worldwide by the media. It was almost as if the real
creators of the formations reacted to the lie by attempting to over-
whelm it with such an astonishing display that no sane person could
deny that some sort of miracle was unfolding.

From then on, the formations have remained complex. For the
most part, they have expressed—or perhaps it is more accurate to say
involved—mathematical, geometric, and musical principles.

It is always useful to remind oneself that a proper pursuit of any
question must of necessity involve paying attention to any available
physical evidence, and the physical evidence that this aspect of it presents is an outburst of artistry that is being disclosed in ephemeral crops.
It is temporary and it must be, because it is being placed in fields
where we are growing plants of economic importance to us. In fact,
some farmers have even reacted to the crop loss with anger, especially
those whose fields are too isolated for them to recoup by charging
tourists, which is the most common way of making up the loss.

They are also concentrated in one of the most ancient areas of
human inhabitation, a region that is filled with sacred sites dating back
to Neolithic times. In the area there are a number of ancient stone
circles, which makes one wonder if they perhaps took as their models
formations that appeared in the fields of their time. The area is also
dotted with mysterious places like the Glastonbury Tor and ancient
places of pilgrimage like the Chalice Well, one of the most beautiful
spots in the world, a humble and yet grand cathedral of nature.

The modern circles are also gathering places. They draw people
from around the world. But they are temporary, and no doubt that fact
is also a message that they won't be here forever. But they are not all
circles. Instead, the formations are complex and suggestive without ever

actually explaining themselves. They are thus not only a gathering place but also a labyrinth of mysteries and questions, tantalizing us to contemplate them and visit them, but never quite revealing a final secret.

The most amazing thing about the formations is that, as ephemeral as they are, each one offers a window into a different deep journey, be it through mathematics, music, or other harmonies. So much is given, a labyrinth that never ends and never ceases to offer rewards. Then the farmer comes and plows his field, the season ends, and all the windows opened that summer on eternal things are closed.

On three occasions, however, formations have appeared that departed from this norm. Instead of offering deep and ambiguous journeys into universal laws, they were almost like news items, speaking directly to the observer. In these cases, they appeared to involve the beings known popularly as the "grays," who dealt directly with me for the first few years of my contact experience. Aliens are not, though—well, there is more to come about these mysterious beings.

When I saw the first of these formations, which appeared close to the Chilbolton Radio Telescope on August 16, 2001, I assumed that it was a hoax. It seemed to be a visual answer to the famous signal broadcast by the Arecibo Radio Telescope in Puerto Rico on November 16, 1974. This signal had contained information about man, our solar system, and planet earth, and was sent in the form of a three-minute transmission that consisted of 1,679 binary digits, chosen because they are a semiprime, or a product of two prime numbers, making decoding a simple process. When they are decoded, as a rectangle consisting of twenty-three columns and seventy-three lines, they produce information in the form of a simple graphic.

This graphic displayed the numbers 1 through 10, the atomic numbers of various elements, the formulas for the sugars and bases in the nucleotides of DNA, the number of nucleotides in DNA, a graphic of a human figure and a symbolic representation of the population of earth, a graphic of the solar system, and one of the Arecibo Radio Telescope.

The graphic that appeared in the Chilbolton field conveyed similar information. The top row of the graphic contains the numbers 1 through 10 in binary form. The next row shows the atomic numbers of the elements hydrogen, carbon, nitrogen, oxygen, and phosphorus. The next four rows contain twelve groups of five numbers each, showing the sugars, bases, and phosphates that make up DNA. There is also a graphic of DNA that is somewhat different from ours, and it has been suggested that subtle differences in the structure of the formation might imply that it was made by a silicon-based life form. There is a cartoon of a figure, as in the Arecibo message, but this one is smaller than a man, and has a very large head.

When I saw it, I reflected that such creatures had been in my old cabin, and had been seen by a number of people there, including one woman, Raven Dana, who touched the hand of one of them. Another man saw one standing beside his bed, but when he felt a shock of fear go through him, its great bulbous head turned into the menacing head of a falcon. So apparently the differences in DNA have produced some rather telling differences not only in morphology but in other ways as well. Did the being actually change shape, something like a startled blowfish, or did it project the change into the witness's mind?

In the Arecibo message, earth is above a line in the solar system, intended to indicate that it is the planet we inhabit. In the Chilbolton graphic, there are four planets above the line, with an arc between two of them. Perhaps one is a moon of the other, meaning that they inhabit three planets and a moon. Certainly, there would need to be a planet with a moon or some other celestial body that would slow rotational winds, or complex life would never have arisen in their solar system. This structure, with a moon rotating at just the right distance to put drag on rotational winds, is essential to variable weather. Without it, a dense atmosphere is going to be dragged by a planet's rotation and generate continuous high winds. On such a world, the evolution of complex life forms would be problematic. In addition, the moon provides a gravitational pull that stabilizes earth's obliquity, or tilt. Without this effect, our climate would cycle between unsurvivable extremes of heat and cold.

In the place where the Arecibo telescope is located in the graphic we transmitted is an image of an enigmatic device of some kind, perhaps something that transmits a beam—and creates crop formations, conceivably.

On balance, the Chilbolton graphic would have been fairly simple to create, although a single mistake would have ruined the whole intricate production. But the enigma didn't stop with the graphic. Just a few yards away, there appeared one of the most unusual formations ever discovered, one that is probably impossible to create using any known means.

For anyone who enjoys puzzles and questions as much as I do, the two formations appearing together were a delicious conundrum very much in keeping with the wry sense of humor that the intelligence that we are involved with has displayed on many occasions.

There were three possibilities to consider. First, perhaps both formations were hoaxes. But frankly, I don't see how the second formation, a face that appeared in the morning of August 14, during a time when no activity was noticed in the field, could have been constructed at all, let alone in a field that was covered by security cameras, without anybody being seen. And the manager of the radio telescope, Darcy Ladd, told researcher Colin Andrews that there had been no unusual activity observed in the field.

In fact, it seems to have just suddenly come there, as if it was stamped out from above—or, perhaps, beamed down.

The optical physics employed in the creation of this face was nothing short of fantastic. It consists of dozens of networks of woven paths and many hundreds of standing cylinders, each one carved out of the wheat with the accuracy necessary to make the face visible from above. Between the cylinders, the wheat on the ground had been woven in such a way as to create the contrasts of light required to generate the image.

So we have two formations side by side in the field, apparently both created on or near August 14, 2001. One of them could conceivably have been hoaxed. The other was constructed by unknown means, and remains perhaps the most spectacularly intricate formation ever seen.

It is of a face, human or almost human, and beside it is a detailed reply to a message we sent out, that suggests that it is from a nonhuman species with small bodies and large heads, a species which might even be silicon- rather than carbon-based. (Silicon is the only other element we know of that might be able to support the complex chemistry of life, but it would be life of a very different kind, one would assume.)

Instead of reacting with curiosity, no scientist at the Chilbolton Radio Telescope reported the formations, even though they were in plain view. They were found by chance by a pilot overflying the area.

Such is the institutional constriction of science that investigation of the formations was left to amateur researchers. They did a very credible job, but as they were without resources, no studies of the soils or the condition of the crops were done, and none of the very precise measurements that would seem appropriate.

One is left to suppose that the scientists at the telescope glanced out at these wonders and said to themselves, "Oh, those two pranksters with boards on their feet have been stomping around in the field."

The face is there either to make it impossible to dismiss the graphic or to in some way give it credence, one would think. Could it be, then, that human beings and this other intelligence worked in concert in that field? Certainly, something like that has happened in my own life. My implant was placed in my ear by people. Were they working with the strange otherworldly beings we had been seeing around the house and in our woods, or against them?

It's impossible to know, but if I may return again to our thought experiment, if we were studying an intelligent species on another planet, it would be of value to us to enlist clandestine cooperation from various local elements. Doctors, biologists, epidemiologists, and engineers might be of interest to us. It might be much easier for us to penetrate deeply into the biology and culture, not to say the individual lives, of the subject species if we could utilize surrogates.

So maybe the face is a kind of stamp of approval of a formation communicating about our visitors that was made by human surrogates who are able to think the same way we think, and were communicating their observations to us from, as it were, behind the line that they had to cross in order to come into direct everyday contact with our visitors.

That would explain why the grammar of the communication is so radically different from the other formations, and so like the way our own minds might work.

One can only speculate, but the fact remains that the Chilbolton formations were written in a different intellectual language than all of the formations that had come before, but not so different from another remarkable formation, which appeared on the night of August 15, 2002, exactly a year after the Chilbolton formation, and just nine miles from its location. It was laid down in a field near Winchester in Hampshire, close to a place called the Crabwood Farm House.

Once again, an entirely human grammar was used, but in a formation so dramatically complex that it is difficult to know how it could have been created with such precision in a dry crop of wheat, let alone by a human hand.

It contained a message that, knowing as much as I did by then about the dark and deceptive side of the experience, was particularly heartening. As you will learn, I have seen some very dark things, some terrible things, and been left not only with questions that delight me but also with some that bring terror to my nights, and dread at the thought of just how alone and helpless we are, lost as we are on this little planet in the great dark.

The formation consisted of a glaring alien face seen in three-quarters profile, and beside it a disk etched into the wheat. I am told by witnesses who visited it when it was fresh that it was completely incomprehensible from the ground. Once again, it was not possible that people on the ground could have carried out the extremely precise measurements needed to make this, not without checking their work from above. And, as always, mistakes could not be corrected.

The first people who entered the formation found that the affected crop was bent above the surface of the soil, so that everywhere they stepped, they left indentations, breaking the brittle stems of the wheat.

This could not have been done by somebody standing on the ground. They would have had to be suspended from above.

It was soon realized that the disk contained a message written in ASCII code, the standard binary code of the type in use in our computers. The message read, "Beware the bearers of false gifts and their broken promises. Much pain but still time. There is good out there. We oppose deception. Conduit closing." After the word "time," there appears the ASCII for "EELIE1366E," but the rest of the message is clearly decipherable.

A number of people who I talked to who had entered the formation told me of a sense of foreboding associated with it—the same thing I'd heard from people who entered the Chilbolton formation the year before. Normally, people who come out of crop formations express a sense of delight.

There have been almost frantic efforts to claim that both of these formations were man-made, but that seems doubtful. One researcher who observed the Chilbolton face on the ground said that it was not only intricate beyond imagining, it was completely impossible to tell what it was without flying above it. And the crop that the Crabwood formation was created in was so dry that it could be crushed almost to powder by a single footstep.

So it can be speculated with some conviction that both formations came about through a mysterious instrumentality.

The scientific response to the whole crop-formation phenomenon can been summed up very neatly by the reaction of the astronomers at the Chilbolton Radio Telescope to the miracle that appeared in the field beside their instrument: they ignored it.

There is really a great deal of research that has been pitifully left undone in those dreaming fields. For example, many fields have had multiple formations appear in them over a period of years, Chilbolton being one such. Is there a progression, perhaps? Something to be learned from the evolution of the forms in a particular location? Or are there larger annular patterns, or some statistical consistency that might be revealed by larger-scale study of the phenomenon?

Is it a communication or not, and if not, what might the formations be for? It is a cruel tragedy that they are not studied, because there must be new knowledge of some sort associated with them, even perhaps knowledge that might lead us to our first insights into the way the truly extraordinary mind behind them works.

To dismiss them as a bunch of drunken pranks, hoaxes, the effects of secret military activities, or the effects of playful winds in the fields is more than just disingenuous, it is not entirely sane. They are simply too fine to be dismissed. But they are also very incomprehensible, and that leads to a sort of terror on the part of any observer who might be able to bring things like mathematical skills to his or her study. It leads to the thought, *My skills are not enough*, and then to the fear, *I am face-to-face with a mind that is really here, and beyond my understanding.*

But is it? Or rather, if the formations are an attempt to communicate with us, perhaps they are not so much beyond comprehension as just strange.

This is not to say that good scientific work hasn't been attempted. As I have mentioned, it has, but it has been directed to attempting to determine some sort of construction methodology, not to a methodical interpretation of the formations. However, it is, in the end, the message that matters.

For example, why are they concentrated in southern England? What is it about this particular area that would attract nearly 90 percent of all crop formations, and by far the greatest number of complex ones? Could we, perhaps by finding their relationship to nearby Neolithic sites, come to some sort of idea, or at least a coherent question, about why they might be here?

On October 12, 1996, *Science News* published a brief article about some findings made by astronomer Gerald Hawkins, who had "noticed that some of the most visually striking of these crop-circle patterns embodied geometric theorems that express specific numerical relationships among the areas of various circles, triangles, and other shapes making up the patterns." Hawkins commented, "These designs demonstrate the remarkable mathematical ability of their creators." He discovered four geometric theorems expressed in the formations, all of them Euclidean, but in 1996 discovered a fifth theorem that was novel. No reference to the theorem has been found, but the circle makers are obviously familiar with it, because they are using it.

Science News concluded, "The persons responsible for this old-fashioned type of mathematical ingenuity remain at large and unknown. Their handiwork flaunts an uncommon facility with Euclidean geometry and signals an astonishing ability to enter fields undetected, to bend living plants without cracking stalks, and to trace out complex, precise patterns, presumably using little more than pegs and ropes, all under cover of darkness."

And there the matter has been left. Without much more engaged institutional support, there is not much to be done that hasn't already been done, and it is by studying large-scale relationships and the progressive nature of the phenomenon as it has moved from simple circles to spectacularly complex designs that insight may perhaps be obtained. But that requires financial resources, and thus the engagement of large institutions.

On the face of it, the progression could be either a learning process or a teaching process, or both. In any case, the fact is that the formations have evolved dramatically over the years, and nobody has made an effort to understand the significance of this evolution.

But it is in the nature of institutions to remain frozen when each individual member has to take a personal risk to direct the whole organization to a novel idea.

What if a professor at a great department of mathematics was to circulate a proposal to study the progressive appearance of mathematical ideas in crop formations over the past thirty years? It's a reasonable enough proposal, but to present it, an individual must put his reputation and his career in jeopardy.

It is not in the nature of institutional organizations to engage in really novel work. Institutions are not adventurers.

So it seems probable that unless some scientist with overwhelming credentials comes forward, the tragic silence will continue, and we will continue to react to the crop formations like uncomprehending chimpanzees sniffing at the wheels of a truck that has come to a stop in their territory.

But we aren't chimpanzees. We can understand the truck. We can understand its cargo. Above all, we can understand the motives of who is getting down from it and entering our world, and the weapons and tools that they carry.

CHAPTER 11
Lost in the Stars

IN SEPTEMBER OF 2010, RENOWNED PHYSICIST Stephen Hawking commented that contact with aliens might be risky and that life-forms advanced enough to reach here might be "nomads, looking to conquer and colonize."

We had better hope not because, as matters stand, and perhaps despite itself, the intelligence that we are facing is probably in control of our future. This is because it is increasingly unlikely that we are going to be able to act decisively enough to prevent our environment from becoming overstressed. If we have not gained an open relationship with them by the time that it does, then what happens to us will be their decision. If they are able to reach out and save us, will they? Or will they let nature take its course?

Our own history is no indicator that the age of a civilization is any measure of its ethical development. In some small part, human history is a chronicle of gradually increasing ethical sensitivity, but it is much more largely a story of the silent suffering of billions who bear brutal elites on their shoulders. Moreover, it is not true that as we have gained social experience, our ethics have consistently increased. Far from it, the Belgian decimation of the Congo, the German genocides, and the genocidal slaughters of Africa all happened in modern times. In fact, in these latter days of our history, as methods of police control and mass murder have been improved, we have been at our most brutal and unethical.

So why should we assume that any other species would be any different? Nevertheless, if our visitors do have the power to save us from a situation like the one we face, and it seems as if they may, it is fair to ask what kind of moral compass they may possess. How ethically developed are they? Do they have compassion, or an ideal of goodness against which they evaluate themselves? Moreover, what are their motives for being here, and how can we expect them to be expressed in the life of our species and our world?

So far, the picture that presents itself is not a simple one, while, as I have said, there is some evidence of compassion, it is also true that there are disturbing elements—very disturbing elements—and I think that concerns such as Dr. Hawking's must be considered carefully.

However, it is also true that contact with our visitors is rarely a straightforward, entirely physical experience like, say, meeting another person. There is always this difference, almost as if the way one looks at a visitor can affect the way in which it is real. One is not a passive participant in an encounter, and not only that, our visitors can control their part of it with exquisite precision. The reasons for this have to do with the way perception affects the assembly of reality. As we are now, we assume that the reality with which we surround ourselves is absolute and immutable, that it affects us rather than flows from us.

Both things seem to be to some extent true, though, and when reading the stories that follow here, it is important to remember that things can be different from how they appear—and, in this case, one hopes that they are. Nevertheless, it is also necessary to understand that no matter how they emerge into our world—and no matter what they are—one thing about our visitors must be true: no matter what they are, their society must be very complex, and, given the intelligence that they demonstrate in their relationship with us, as individuals they must also be quite complex. We can expect at least as much variability among them as there is among us.

For example, some books have been published suggesting that most close encounters are similar, but this is really very far from true. In the book *The Communion Letters*, edited by Anne Strieber, 115 accounts show the amazing variety of experience that's out there. And most of these accounts come from natural memory. They have not been enhanced or distorted by hypnosis. The only consistency among them is the extreme care the visitors take that they leave no proof behind—either because they are operating under a general stricture of secrecy or, perhaps, because they can't, for reasons that I will discuss in a later chapter.

The complexity and variety of the encounter experiences being reported doesn't necessarily mean that our visitors are an older civilization, or even that they have any sort of social order that would be familiar to us. What it means is that they're highly intelligent, but not necessarily that they possess a high and ancient culture, or even a low culture, for that matter.

In face-to-face encounter with them, there is no sense of any shared humanity at all. Raven Dana, during a face-to-face encounter in our old cabin, said that at first she thought she was looking at "an animal." She thought the small, spindly creature with the huge eyes that was crouched at the foot of her bed was a raccoon that had come in the window. Then she remembered that the window screen was screwed closed. (I had long since had all the screens sealed in this way.) Then she reached out and touched hands with it, marking one of the few moments I know of when a person in full normal consciousness has touched one of these creatures in an entirely normal manner.

I understood why she'd reacted at first as if it was an animal, because the few direct physical encounters I'd had in our woods had all started the same way. My mind would leap to the thought that I was seeing an animal.

One piece of evidence that does suggest that we might be dealing with a civilization is the consistent way in which our visitors guard their secrecy. Only on the very rarest occasion, for example, has one of them appeared in a public place. The stories of Councilor Hicks, Bruce Lee, and Timothy Greenfield-Sanders, while not unique, are among a very few.

Over the years, I have never been far from bizarre stories about them, and some of these are not as droll and charming as Councilor Hicks's. While few of the hundreds of thousands of letters we received after I published *Communion* described negative experiences, some did, and they were harrowing, and they must not be ignored simply because we find it difficult to face them.

One man told how he had experienced a sort of annihilation in the middle of the night, as if his head had exploded and "I had disappeared." A noise began above the house, and he felt as if something was trying to drag his consciousness out of his body. With his wife holding him, and the noise continuing, the struggle went on for three hours.

A woman, a schoolteacher, looked up from vacuuming her living room to find herself face-to-face with a creature resembling the one on the cover of *Communion*. It demanded that she "come with us." She refused to go, and found herself crawling away in her desperate effort to escape. The next thing she knew, she was at her husband's feet. He'd come home and saved her. But then the creature was there again. It had been an illusion designed to break her will, and it did. She experienced over an hour of lost time. She was never able to recover any memory of what may have happened to her. I talked to her extensively, and she certainly believed that this had happened.

In another case, a man noticed what appeared to him to be children lingering around a lake on his estate. When they wouldn't leave, he went down to the lake with a shotgun. After hearing a loud noise and seeing him fall, his family ran down to find him collapsed, the shotgun unfired, and not a mark on his body. He was dead. There was a rectangular object under the skin of his chest, which was removed during autopsy, and which the family never saw again. Inexplicably, they found their lake to be filled with salmon, which had never been there before.

A fourth case involved two women who went stargazing late at night. As they were getting out of the car in an isolated area north of Vancouver, they were appalled to see three pairs of slanted, lime-green eyes glowing in the beam of their flashlight. They thought that these were animals of some sort, and began to return to the car. But they were not animals. They came to the car window, peering in. The next thing the women knew, forty-five minutes had passed. Both had received injuries and required medical attention. This happened in the context of an extensive UFO wave taking place in the area at the time. Once again, the women were unable to recover any memories of their experience.

The vast majority of the accounts I received told of perplexing and disturbing experiences rather than terrible ones, though. In fact, my own remains one of the most difficult I have heard described.

Not as difficult, though, as the ones that involve the death of the witness. In all the letters we received, the only one where a death is mentioned is the one involving the man with the shotgun.

That is not true in the general literature, though.

On August 2, 2002, a thirty-eight-year-old man called Todd Sees set out to find possible sites from which to hunt deer in a Pennsylvania woodland. When he failed to return after two days, his wife finally called police. A search was instituted and Mr. Sees's four-wheel off-road vehicle was found. One of his shoes was found nearby. Dogs were brought in, but they could not pick up his scent anywhere but on the bike itself.

Allegedly, a local man had seen a UFO along the ridge and a body rising into it, but this story was never confirmed. A Mutual UFO Network investigator, attorney Wayne Gracey, did speak to a woman who had observed a silver disk in the area at approximately the time of the disappearance, but she did not report seeing any movement around it.

Mr. Sees was eventually found dead in a wetland a short distance from his home. He was wearing only boxer shorts and had his hands to his throat as if he had been choking. A dead rattlesnake was found beside the body, but there was no evidence of a snakebite.

How Mr. Sees negotiated the rough woodlands above the Susquehanna River in nothing but a pair of boxer shorts is unknown, and the rest of his clothing was never found.

The police were unwilling to discuss the case, and there were various rumors about the condition of the body. Eventually a toxicology report was issued stating that Mr. Sees had died of a cocaine overdose. There were also stories about him being stung to death by bees.

Despite the fact that this closed the case, police and the coroner have been unwilling to release any further reports, or to say why they would not.

In the UFO community, there was speculation that he had died after being mutilated by the same mysterious presence that has been mutilating cattle, mostly in the western United States, at least since the 1970s. But it was only speculation, and no more hard information could be obtained—primarily the testimony of professionals who had seen the body, and, above all, the autopsy and toxicology reports.

Two years later, I received correspondence from an individual who claimed to know a coroner in the same general area, who had autopsied a number of corpses of people who had been bizarrely mutilated. I was told that there had been seventeen cases, all involving homeless people who had been taken from the streets of small cities in the area, tortured by mutilation, drowned in the ocean, and their bodies then returned to locations near where they had first been kidnapped.

Their injuries showed that they had been mutilated while alive, and then died after being taken down to a considerable depth, probably in excess of a hundred feet. Their lungs contained salt water and had received pressure damage.

While these descriptions were vivid and detailed, I was never able to confirm them, because the person who was giving me the information wouldn't put me in touch with the coroner involved.

So what might this have meant? My personal experience of close encounter had moved from rough treatment to experiences more sublime, which I will relate, than any I have read of, because they opened a window for me into a new world, and did this without confusing matters with mythological trappings. What happened to me as the veil that seems to surround human experience was lifted was not filled with awesome symbolism. I didn't see the face of God. What I saw in my excursion into higher life was hard work being done with skill and care, in a context that was far beyond anything I had previously known or expected.

Nevertheless, it is absolutely essential to me that I not turn away from these dark events, nor pretend they didn't happen, nor engage in some facile dismissal.

I don't know whether they happened or not. Perhaps the Todd Sees case is simply a matter of a man who got himself killed wandering in the woods. Maybe the wave of mutilations across northern New Jersey and New York never happened, and I was simply the victim of a paranoid and his delusions.

I cannot know the answers to these questions, but I do know that animals have suffered mutilations for years. Author Charles Fort, in his book *Lo!*, describes widespread surgical mutilation of sheep in Wales in 1904 to 1905, commenting that they took place after a religious revival swept the region. Whether they were connected or not isn't clear, but he relates that there were strange lights seen at the time, which is also a characteristic of the modern animal-mutilation phenomenon.

Modern ranchers consistently report seeing lights in distant fields prior to finding mutilated cattle, and they were seen again in Wales beginning in 2009, when sheep mutilations returned to the area after an absence of 105 years.

In March of 2009, members of the British Animal Pathology Field Unit were called to a farm in Radnor Forest in Wales, where the bloodless corpses of four ewes had been discovered. In January and February of 2010, they returned to the same farm to investigate the discovery of three more sheep mutilations, once again with all the blood removed from the carcasses.

In April of 2010, a dozen sheep were discovered to have been butchered in a bizarre way on a farm in Hamsterley, Durham, in northern England.

Unidentified red-orange spheres have also been reported in the area, just as was true in 1904 to 1905.

Investigator Phil Hoyle told reporter Linda Moulton Howe, "The animals (sheep) were having complete facial strips and other organs and tissue removed with no blood loss. In the Radnor Forest, Radnorshire region, there is a history of very unusual activity and also a massive amount of military surveillance—actually illegal surveillance—because some of the helicopters are American-built Apache helicopters. We have video of them virtually *touching the roof* of a farmhouse and monitoring around the area constantly."

So, yet again, there is the impression of military activity in the area of unexplained events. But, as always, exactly what is being done and by whom isn't clear.

Mr. Hoyle continues, "People tell me they have seen things they could not explain and tell me they have seen orange spheres that have come at night to the wooded areas where there are small pools and reservoirs. The people have the distinct impression that these spheres are actually drawing water from the pools."

The relationship between these strange objects and bodies of water has been observed for a long time, and in his seminal book *The Fairy-Faith in Celtic Countries*, Walter Evans-Wentz comments that one of the believers he interviewed said, "They never taste anything salt, but eat fresh meat and pure water."

Given the butchering of the sheep and the taking of the water, it looks as if "they" were supplying themselves with both in Wales, a historical center of the fairy-faith, in 2009 and 2010.

Linda Moulton Howe, who has been investigating these cases for many years, comments on her website, Earthfiles.com, that "the orange spheres are also what I encountered in my interviews with law enforcement and ranchers from 1979 onward in my own animal mutilation investigations in the United States and Canada."

The recent sheep kills in the United Kingdom followed two patterns. First, there were the animals on the farm in Wales, which exhibited classic signs of the mutilations: the removal of all blood from the body; the coring out of genitals, eyes, and rectum; smooth, surgical excisions of flesh from around the jaw and other areas of the body. This pattern has been repeated in thousands of cases worldwide.

Generally, animal mutilations are dismissed as the work of predators. The surgical quality of the damage is ignored and the disappearance of the blood is simply dismissed. Nevertheless, it is not likely that this is the case, and to prove this it is necessary only to examine the condition of the eye sockets.

Birds will remove eyes from their prey, but they will do this by pulling with their claws and tearing and pecking with their beaks. The eyes of mutilated animals are removed lid and all, and there is a cut around the socket where a bit of flesh has been taken as part of the surgery. Not only that, there is a nutrition-rich pad of fat behind the eye that is a primary objective of predators, but it is always left behind in surgically mutilated animals.

So, once again, we have a situation where something is being arbitrarily dismissed that is clearly not what it seems. To some degree, modern events seem related to things that were reported by believers in the fairy-faith, but prior to the twentieth century, there are not many specific reports of animal mutilations, only the assertion among believers that the fairy-folk preferred "fresh meat."

The modern animal-mutilation phenomenon is not confined to horses and food animals. Housecats are also very commonly mutilated, and these cases are not only extraordinarily brutal, they are cruel not only to the animals but to the people who love them.

In 1978 in St. Catherine's near Toronto, over a hundred cats and dogs went missing, and more were found dead, usually in their owner's yards, mutilated and skinned, with the blood entirely gone. Some had been decapitated, others cut in half; others had their paws missing. No trace of the blood was ever found.

For the more than thirty years since, such events have been reported in Canada, the United States, the United Kingdom, and other places. There is no way to tell how many have gone unreported—say, when only one or two animals are affected, or the animals simply disappear.

Generally, the remains, or some of the remains, are returned to the area where the animal was taken, in an eerie reminder of what was done in the abduction/mutilation/drowning cases referred to above. The butchery is neat, and the incisions in some cases appear to have been accomplished with some sort of laser. When Ms. Howe took a half-cat corpse to Dr. John Altshuler in Denver, he found that the "entire excision had been cut with something hot enough to cook the collagen and hemoglobin."

Laser scalpels are used in ophthalmology, neurosurgery, and vascular surgery, but the precision instruments that are generally available would not be appropriate to cut a cat in half.

She further reports that the supervisor of animal control for the

Vancouver City Pound said, "The cats are clearly being butchered by someone. It's a real surgical job."

Of course, it's easy enough to ascribe these attacks to some sort of cult or twisted individuals, but can that be correct? Thousands have been reported, spread across half the world, and despite intense police investigations in many cities, not a single piece of evidence has been found that points toward any suspects.

This is also true, incidentally, of the cattle and sheep mutilations. Despite the fact that they have been going on for at least a hundred years and have taken place in at least a dozen countries, there has never been a single suspect apprehended, and the only unusual evidence that has been consistently observed, aside from the mutilated animals, are strange lights.

There is one human–mutilation case from Brazil where there is a significant amount of evidence. Some disturbing photos of a body that had been found near Guarapiranga Reservoir on September 29, 1988, made their way to researchers who recognized the wounds displayed as being similar to those on mutilated cattle. The head of the forensic investigation, a Dr. Cuenca, made his report available, and it, along with the photographs, were published in the Brazilian magazine *UFO*. The autopsy report states, "There has been a removal of extensive tissue along many parts of the face, head and neck of the victim. . . . There has also been extraction of ocular tissue, eyes, auditive internal and external organs (ears) and entire parts of the head. The tongue and several muscles were also extracted."

The eyes appear to have been removed in the same way that the eyes of mutilated cattle are removed, excised using a cutting tool rather than being pulled out by a predator.

Of course, in this case, as in all the cattle mutilations, there is no way to say definitively that the mutilations were not done by lunatics or cultists of some sort.

However, it seems essential that some more serious effort be made to investigate such cases, and that there be a level of assurance, lacking at present, that laboratories will provide truthful and accurate results when asked, for example, to analyze tissue.

Misleading laboratory findings have been a problem. In late 1975, the Colorado Bureau of Investigation (CBI) started a process of laboratory investigation of the remains of mutilated animals, and soon began reporting that most were clearly the result of predator attacks. According to Linda Moulton Howe, one sheriff was not satisfied with this conclusion, and sent the CBI samples that he and his deputies had personally cut from a cow carcass using sharp knives. The report came back that the cuts had been made by a predator, and even included the information that a fox hair had been found on the sample. Given that foxes had long since disappeared from the area and the cuts were made by a man with a knife, this seems an improbable conclusion.

But it does point out something I have learned from my own research: laboratories are not necessarily to be trusted, so profound is the tendency to reject this reality.

Undoubtedly, a technician took one look at the sample, realized that it had been cut in some sort of surgery, and thought, *If I say that, my superiors aren't going to like it*, and chose the comfortable lie.

And he was probably right to do so, at least as far as his job security was concerned.

In his book *Confrontations*, Dr. Jacques Vallée discusses a number of other cases from Brazil that also took place in the 1980s. Two of them involved the death of witnesses. One of them, a hunter, died suddenly after a nighttime deer hunt, in an area where other witnesses had seen lights. There was nothing to connect him directly with them, but there were "round, red-purple, smooth marks on the neck, about one and a quarter inch in diameter." They were on either side of the neck, about two inches below the ear. The victim was forty years old and in good health, so there was no obvious explanation for his death. Unfortunately, the family did not authorize an autopsy, so the case is no more than suggestive, and Dr. Vallée has said that he does not think it was related to a UFO encounter.

In another case, a hunter named Raimundo Souza, also forty, was hunting at night with a friend when he was mysteriously killed. This death occurred during the 1981–1982 UFO wave in Brazil. Souza and a hunting companion, Anastasio Barbosa, were waiting for game one night when Souza struck a match.

Immediately, a lighted object came down out of the sky and hovered over them, aiming a beam of light at them. Barbosa crept under some bushes and remained there for the rest of the night. Souza did not hide. When daylight came, Barbosa discovered him dead.

His body had several purple marks on it. One of his arms was broken, as if at some point he had fallen from the hammock he had been lying in. Again, there was no autopsy, so there can be no definite conclusions regarding the case. He may have simply fallen.

Vallée reports that there were many cases involving a bright beam of light shining on witnesses, but no other deaths that he was able to discover. Some people did report being drained of strength by the light.

Such cases were reported during a significant UFO wave in islands near Belém in 1977. They happened between July and September of that year, on the islands of Mosqueiro and Colares and at a beach known as the Beach of the Sun.

Objects were appearing over the area regularly at the time. They were photographed. The Brazilian military attempted communication. And people who were struck by the beams of light they emitted began appearing at the hospital.

Dr. Wellaide Cecim Carvalho de Oliveira, the director of the community health center on the archipelago of Marajó, found that the patients all exhibited similar symptoms, among them extreme weakness, dizziness, numbness, low blood pressure, low hemoglobin levels, and blackened skin where the light had hit them. Some also had painful red-purple circles, conceivably similar to those found in the cases of the two dead hunters.

The doctor also found inside the red circles puncture marks that were hard to the touch and resembled mosquito bites, and observed that hair in the blackened areas of skin fell out and did not regrow, as if follicle destruction had occurred.

One symptom that all of her patients—about twenty people in total—all shared was a drop in red blood cells.

They all had told the same story. They had been in their hammocks at night when a light hit them from above and immobilized them. The beam was intolerably hot but would soon retract. With two exceptions the victims recovered fully. One died, apparently of a heart attack after being hit by the light.

Interestingly, the doctor herself had a spectacular UFO sighting, "the most beautiful thing I have ever witnessed."

It was described as "a brilliant, large cylinder with purple lights at the top and bottom, shining in concentric rings." It "flew low over the street" and drew an enthusiastic crowd of townspeople as it danced and darted through the sky, and they shouted, banged drums and cans, and blew off fireworks.

There were many photographs taken during this UFO wave, but no negatives are available. They were all purchased from newspapers all over the country by an American firm that nobody has ever been able to trace.

Before leaving the dark continent of negative UFO-related events and going on to the flowering of my own experience that took place in the 1990s and that I have never before reported, we must move to the present day and travel from Brazil to Sulawesi and the district of Sandu Batu.

In May of 2010, my website, Unknowncountry.com, received a

communication from Alan Lamers, who was a specialist in creating small, self-powered radio stations for isolated rural communities and was working in the area.

He had a good command of the local language, and considerable experience in deep rural areas of Indonesia and other countries with extremely isolated populations, so when he was told a few years ago that he would disappear if he wore bright colors when going to a tiny, off-the-map village called Wala Wala, he assumed that there was a local taboo.

Once in the village, he saw that the locals were all wearing only black or white. Nobody would say why.

Everyone in Alan's party was wearing black, except one man who had not understood the instructions and had on yellow socks. That afternoon, they went into the jungle for a time, and when they came back the man was uneasy. Something that he could not see had scratched his leg. When he pulled off his socks, the scratches were found to be large.

The villagers said the man was lucky to have just been scratched. Usually, they said, people wearing colored clothing into the jungle do not return.

The man who had been scratched endured fever and they thought they would lose him, but he eventually recovered. They could not find out from the villagers exactly what was wrong, beyond the fact that many people had disappeared in the jungle. These people are living in very isolated country. There are no roads, only trails. Big population centers might as well be on another planet.

In May of 2010, Alan finally learned more about the mysterious danger confronted by those by wearing bright colors in the jungles of the district. He had gone to visit a friend in the city of Palopo and discovered that her cousin knew a considerable amount about the problem.

It seems that her brother had gone hiking with friends, and the entire party had disappeared.

She eventually hired a search-and-rescue team, but nobody could be found, and it was assumed that they had met with some sort of misadventure in the jungle. This was unusual, as it was a tourist area, and Indonesia is regarded as a relatively safe place. They didn't disappear in the deep jungle, amid profound isolation.

After a month of searching, they found the brother exhausted and emaciated. He was severely traumatized, and did not speak for two more months. Alan talked to him briefly, but he began to return to his silence, so he asked the sister what he had told her.

He wrote me, "There is something taking these people, Whitley, something terrible and evil. The people have come to terms with it and have tried to adapt themselves to deal with whatever it is."

He discovered that it has been going on for years, and local people, Muslims, assume that the culprits are djinn.

He continued, "I found out he kept seeing what the Bugis call Jin Kurcaci. It means little demon people. These things do what is called 'penculikan' or abduction. No one knows why they do this. But sometimes the people come back after a bit. The people or creatures who do this have a small nose and their eyes are small and black, but their mouths are very broad and when they smile it is very large compared to the rest of their face."

As they hiked, they seemed to enter another sort of world. They could see animals with antlers unlike anything on Sulawesi. The young man does not remember exactly what happened to his friends, but he does recall being given food and being sent back to warn people—apparently by the same sort of creatures who were causing the disappearances, perhaps some that disagree with what the others are doing.

The fairy lore of northern Europe is full of stories of disappearances, but the victims almost always return.

So what might it all mean? What might any of it mean?

From UFO displays to crop circles to implants to bizarre attacks, what we are looking at is a mystery so huge that it is almost too big to see, which is probably why its many different aspects are usually dealt with separately.

Whether they are all part of the same phenomenon or not it is impossible to tell, but all of these mysteries are linked in one particular way: they are all denied.

UFOs are explained away as secret aircraft even though anyone with the slightest grasp of the history of this part of the phenomenon would know that this is utterly false. In the 1760s, a massive UFO wave over Japan caused so much unrest that it nearly toppled the government, and the descriptions of the objects were very similar to many that are seen today: great balls of light alternatively hovering and whipping through the sky at fantastic speeds. Eighteenth-century Japanese astronomers managed to calm things down with the first known official denial of the reality of this mystery. They explained that what people were seeing was "the wind making the stars sway."

So much more poetic than swamp gas, and no less believable.

Crop formations—that immense outpouring of subtle grandeur, at once vivid with meaning and impenetrably exotic—are laughed off as the production of drunks with boards on their feet.

Cattle mutilations are lied about by laboratories. The true extent of human mutilations is so well concealed that it can barely even be approached. Implants are ignored or explained away as things like bits of stone people have stepped on. But the same people who explain them away fail to mention that most of the ones that have been studied are made of the same substance—meteoric iron. Why would people be stepping on meteoric iron, and how would the bits travel from their feet into their wrists or arms or jaws, or emit radio signals? It's never explained.

A gigantic event is unfolding, and from UFO sightings to cattle mutilations to implants and all the rest, the response is uniform: denial of the facts, and compromise to the reputation of anybody who speaks out.

Is there some sort of hidden dictatorship governing this bizarre behavior? It's impossible to believe that this much evidence could be ignored, but it is, and not only ignored but dismissed with absurd lies that—incredibly—work.

Since I published *Communion*, I have lived a strange, marginalized life, and have been lied about, laughed at, and shoved aside. But why? I have provided a reasonably articulate description of some very unusual and challenging experiences, and, rather than announcing that I've had alien contact or whatever, offered a clear set of questions about them.

In my ridiculous martyrdom, though, I am hardly alone. Every single person who has done serious research in this field has been similarly shoved into the ghetto of "UFO believer," and lumped with those who are unable to bear the question and have, in the absence of any clear institutional leadership and serious study, woven mostly silly stories around the phenomenon in order to relieve the tension of not knowing. So you have the serious researchers buried beneath a mountain of reptilians, Zetas, Pleiadians, Deros, and other folkloric beings, and their work considered in the same light as the fantasy and hearsay.

As I have said, most of the researchers believe that we are looking at the work of creatures from another planet. Personally, I wonder if there is not a more thorough and accurate way of describing what is happening.

Throughout this book, I have used the model of our own hypothetical visit to another world. What would we do? How would we engage in our studies? And I have shown that, to a great extent, what our visitors do here is an exact parallel to what we would do if the roles were reversed.

But when it comes to attacks and mutilations, the metaphor

collapses. This chapter is a chronicle of some sort of madness, not the gentle probing of curious aliens, but a rapacious, crazed attack.

Fortunately for the rest of us, the great majority of these cases are concentrated in isolated areas. I have touched here on only a few of them. There are many, many more, of people being set upon by lighted objects in the night and dragged into them, sometimes with beams of light, other times with actual hooks. The only cases we have, of course, are of those who weren't successfully taken. How many may have disappeared from isolated parts of places like Brazil nobody knows.

Nevertheless, there is knowledge to be had here, even from these dark stories. For example, next to the crop formations, the cattle mutilations are probably the most extensive evidentiary resource available to students of this mystery.

UFOs that buzz around like flies but won't engage with us. Sublime crop formations laid down by a genius hand in the fields of England— but beyond our understanding. People mysteriously implanted with devices we also don't understand. Cattle brutally tortured and killed in mad rituals. People disappearing into a demon-choked fog in isolated back-country.

What manner of mind creates such a bizarre combination of events?

The contrasts in the contact experience are fantastic. For example, some of the cases studied in Brazil appear horrifying. It seems possible that there are even worse ones that are unknown. By contrast, relatively few of the letters we received described anything brutal and, as I have said, only one involved a death.

Could it be that our world is divided into territories? How differently might New Zealanders and North Koreans treat our helpless alien subjects on their vulnerable planet? Or the Mexicans and the Mongolians, or the Scientologists and the Catholics? Or what if anybody could go, and it wasn't even very expensive? Would serial killers go? Ritual murderers? Some human visitors would certainly be more exploitative than others.

In the years after my close encounter, I gradually ceased to see the little beings I had come to think of as my visitors. Instead, in the winter of 1990, somebody new showed up at my cabin, somebody so incredible that his mere existence upended my understanding of reality yet again, and I found myself facing the true vastness of the question, in the cold of a winter's night, with the snow whispering down.

PART THREE

Caterpillar and Butterfly: Lifting the Veil

AT THIS POINT, WE VENTURE BEYOND THE FRON-
tiers of physical evidence, and also of the ability of
science as it is presently constituted to investigate.
Here, we will come face-to-face with the intelligence
that has involved itself with us, and see flickers of personality, resonant
depth, and an eerie echo of our own being.

At the beginning of this book, I suggested that something is wrong,
and what it is should now be quite clear. The close-encounter experience is a chaos of contradictions. Most of what we can see about it
is either horrific beyond words filled with wonder, or won't ever quite
come into focus.

So far, very few attempts at communication have worked. No official efforts—at least, none that are known—have been successful.

In 1952 there was an extensive UFO wave over the eastern half of
the United States. It included the appearance of bizarre and monstrous
forms on a rural Kentucky farm, extensive UFO overflights over many
states, and even Paul Hill's first UFO sighting. There was a wave of UFO
sightings over Washington, infamously explained away as "swamp
gas."

But no communication.

In the 1977 Brazil wave, a UFO actually landed in a field in the presence of Brazilian military, who sought to communicate with it. But when they ran toward it, the thing skittered away like a frightened rabbit.

Again, no communication.

My own effort was perhaps moderately successful, though, and I think that I have understood the reasons for this success. Certainly, unless we can learn to communicate with our visitors, there will be no way out of the labyrinth we are in, and our confusion is apt to get worse, not better.

Sixty years ago, there had been cattle mutilations. Forty years ago, there were no reported abductions. Twenty years ago, no reports of human mutilations. Two years ago, no stories like the one out of Sulawesi.

This is not a good progression. I hesitate to think what might happen if worse things start unfolding elsewhere, or over the entire world. Then the thing is done: earth will have become hell.

What happens to the disappeared, and for those of us who are not simply taken, what does it mean to be affected by the visitors? And how, in the midst of all this darkness, have I found the new strength of spirit that has come into my life?

Does my journey suggest the beginnings, perhaps, of some sort of useful reaction to what seems a deranged and potentially predatory presence, a way out of the underworld?

I am willing to hope that it does.

In 1985, I entered a place darker and more terrible than I could ever have imagined. More than once, I came close to joining the disappeared.

I am not there now. I have come to an accommodation with my own phantoms that seems much more promising.

Let me tell you how.

CHAPTER 12
Deliverance

O N A SNOWY AFTERNOON IN MARCH OF 1985, Anne and I closed on our cabin in upstate New York. It was a modest little place, two bedrooms down and one up. After the sale closed, we drove down to it under darkening skies, and installed a few lightbulbs.

Surely we were safe in the deep country. Here there were no muggers, no murders. Just a few months before, I had surprised a pair of men in the act of pulling out a knife as they came up behind us in a subway station. Fortunately, they ran. Not here, though. Not in the empty woods.

But as we worked in the cabin, I felt a creeping uneasiness. As the darkness grew deeper, the feeling intensified.

We were no strangers to dark mysteries. When we were first married, we lived in a tiny apartment on West Fifty-fifth Street in Manhattan. Walking to and from our jobs, we often passed a storefront on what was a quiet stretch of the street between Eighth Avenue and Broadway. There was no sign on the storefront. In the store window was a chair. Behind it, a dark green curtain.

Every so often, there would be a girl sitting in the chair. She was always impeccably dressed, looking as if she'd just come from Fifth Avenue. It never seemed to be the same girl twice, and they always looked as if they were ashamed to be there. They sat staring straight ahead. Nobody entered the store, nobody left.

We thought they were prostitutes, and we laughingly called it "the whore store," but even when I passed by alone, there was not the slightest come-hither. Simply sitting, staring.

Then, one night, Anne and I were walking home from Doubleday's bookstore on Fifth Avenue. It was perhaps nine in the evening, and things were not as usual in the whore store.

The curtain was flapping and it appeared that a man in a suit was trying to get out from behind it. What was so terribly odd, though, was that small, dark blue figures kept appearing, racing out from behind the curtain and back again, while the man struggled to get away.

For a moment, it seemed funny. Blue dwarfs? Then the coldest chill came over me. I looked at Anne. Her eyes were wide. She slowly shook her head, and I knew that this was all wrong, this could not be.

We ran. We never looked back. We never went past that place again, not by day or night, alone or together. When we wanted to walk toward the East Side, we went down another street.

We never found out what had happened there that night. At the time, of course, we knew nothing about things like UFOs and aliens. What had been quite a feature of my childhood had by now been dismissed entirely, dismissed and forgotten.

The mind seems to encapsulate memories too strange to understand, then to erase them. Only when similar events recur do they resurface. I will never forget, when I was under hypnosis with Dr. Donald Klein and describing a close encounter, he asked me, "How old are you?" To my amazement, I heard my child's voice pipe up in its Texas accent, "Twelve."

He had noticed that as I was describing the encounter, my voice had changed. From long experience, he knew that the mind, remembering recent trauma, might spontaneously return to memories of older experiences that have become buried.

But in the early seventies, it was all buried. I had no sense of familiarity about what we were seeing. My only thought was that it was scary and it was wrong, and something terrible was happening to that man.

It wasn't until many years later that I would see such creatures again, on the night of my close encounter, working busily to carry me and restrain me. Others have seen them too, always working, short, broad, and wearing dark blue uniforms covered with pockets and flaps.

A psychologist wrote me some years ago, telling me of a remarkable event he had witnessed on the Grand Central Parkway across from LaGuardia Airport. I met him and we discussed his experience. He had been driving along the traffic-filled parkway when he had seen what appeared to be a huge jet at low altitude coming toward his car. He was appalled, and started trying to get out of the traffic stream. But then it passed overhead, and as it did, he was perplexed to see that it looked like some sort of a fake airplane, like a stage prop.

The next thing he saw was even stranger. In full view of the early evening traffic, an enormous lighted sign on the roadside was flashing what appeared to be a coded message. More incredibly, cars were stopping on the roadside and people were getting out. Fascinated, he stopped his car. On the roadside, he could see a group of people standing in a circle. As he walked up to them, a small figure appeared, dressed in dark blue. His impression was of some kind of a circus clown. The clown was tough, though, and snarled at him to go away, and he did.

These are far from the only events that imply that the close-encounter experience is more deeply embedded in our world than we imagine. But given the social opprobrium, not many people are going to be willing to come forward, and it would seem, perhaps, that many of them have, in any case, no memory of this part of their lives.

I know people who have had close-encounter experiences among witnesses, then later entirely forgotten them. The mind buries these memories, and with them, perhaps, a whole aspect of human life that is entirely unsuspected.

Are our visitors not visitors at all but something else, perhaps as alien to us as a butterfly would be to a caterpillar?

One witness whom I have known for years, Lorie Barnes, was surprised by these blue creatures back in the 1950s. It was evening, and she was alone at home, reading in bed. She was pregnant. A movement near her bed caused her to look up, and she was startled to see a group of what appeared to be dark blue dwarfs that looked like frogs. Naturally, she was terrified. The one closest to her laid a hand on hers and said, "Do not fear. We are not here for you. We are interested in the girl child you are carrying."

At that time, there was no way to tell the sex of a child until it was born. The baby was indeed a girl, and she has grown up to be a skilled professional without the slightest interest in little men, blue, green, or otherwise.

Lorie then cried out, "You're so ugly!" The leader spoke again. He said, "One day, my dear, you will look just like us."

Could it be that caterpillars find butterflies hideous?

The close-encounter experience is in some way part of human life. I don't know how common it is, but I feel almost certain that it has been woven into our lives for a long time.

As well as anecdotes like these, the stories of the gentry and the fairy-folk related by Evans-Wentz suggest as much. And remember, please, that the "little people" were not regarded as cute little sprites until the sentimentalists of the late nineteenth and early twentieth centuries reinvented them.

In the old days, they were an ominous and often dangerous presence, sometimes bringing gifts but as often also danger and fear and disappearance. People who went with them would sometimes never return, or would come back years later thinking that only moments had passed. It's not for nothing that the old lullaby says, "Gang away peerie femries, come doon bonny angels, to our little room."

In our young years, Anne and I actually had two little rooms on the top floor of an old building on Fifty-fifth Street near Ninth Avenue. That apartment was our little love nest, and I remember it fondly, but I don't remember some of the things that happened there with anything but disquiet, and the knowledge that I really should break myself of the habit of calling the entities I have been connected with all these years "visitors." They are hardly visitors. With all their strangeness, with the danger and fear they have brought, and the loving way they have cherished me and taught me, they have been with me, in fact, all of my life. Whatever they are and wherever they are from, the most true things I know about them are two: they are here, and they are part of human life.

One Saturday afternoon we were in our apartment, listening to music on the portable stereo that had been with me from college days. The record had stopped, but the amplifier was still on when suddenly a voice said through the speakers, "Whitley."

We both looked across the room. Had the stereo just spoken?

"Whitley," it said again. It sounded like the voice of a man in his thirties or forties.

"Who are you?" I asked.

"I know who you are," it replied.

We looked at each other. We weren't experts. Could somebody talk to us through our stereo? We weren't sure.

"I know you're married," it said. It paused, then it said, "Hello, Anne."

Now I was scared and more than a little angry. One of our neighbors must be playing a joke on us. Not a funny joke, though.

"Who are you?" I asked more sharply.

"I know something else about you," it said.

"What? *What?*"

It never spoke again. We unplugged the stereo.

On Monday, I called the Federal Communications Commission to complain about the interference. In that very different world, I was put through to somebody who knew about such things, and he assured me that the only interference my stereo might have picked up would have been from a passing cab or maybe a police car. I would hear the driver's voice, conceivably, communicating with his base station. But he would never be able to hear me.

I protested that somebody had conversed with me. "Then," the man said, "there must be a microphone somewhere."

We couldn't find one, and the stereo didn't have one in it.

Then, one night, I was taking out the garbage when I heard a peculiar sound on the floor below us. I went downstairs and to my horror ended up face-to-face with the sickest man I had ever seen.

He was so thin he was almost skeletonized. He looked like a concentration camp victim. His eyes were dark hollows and he appeared to be grimacing. Frankly, his face looked like something out of a horror film.

When he saw me, he began moving toward me. This explained the sound, because he would move not by walking but by thrusting his midriff forward with his legs spread, causing him to slide along the floor in jerks.

His eyes bored into me. Closer, his face appeared to be decayed.

I ran upstairs and locked the door. After a time, the slipping, sliding noise came to it, then fell silent. We hid in that apartment like a couple of terrified little mice.

The next day, I began to investigate. I asked the neighbors if they'd ever seen him. Nobody had. I didn't have the guts to knock on his door, but I went down to the alley and looked up at his windows.

I was shocked and horrified to see that they were all boarded up with plywood. New plywood, still fresh and golden. They had not been boarded up for long.

I thought he must have some horrific skin disease. I worried about infection. I wanted to know more.

But when I telephoned the landlord, he told me that the apartment was vacant. I said that it was not vacant. There was somebody there and they had boarded up the windows.

A couple of nights later, there was another peculiar sound outside our door, a long, expiring hiss, like something dragging itself along the floor.

A few minutes later, I heard voices rising in the hallway. I opened our door a crack, and the voices got louder. People were yelling up and down the halls. I called back to Anne, "I think there's a fire."

Then I opened the door wider and stepped out, and immediately realized that the yelling was not about a fire.

There were great smears of blood on the walls of the hallway. It was gleaming wet, black in the fluorescent light, in places dripping to the floor. It led down all eight flights of stairs and out the front of the building.

The police had been called and we tenants gathered in the lobby, afraid to return to our apartments. The police checked out the roof, the halls, the basement, but nothing unusual was discovered except for the blood itself.

The next day, men were there cleaning it up. I noticed that they took the boards off the windows of the apartment below ours. I went down and looked in. It was empty, rather dusty. That was all.

We never found out another thing about the squatter. Nobody but me had apparently even seen him.

Not long after that, we moved. I could no longer get a peaceful night's sleep there. To this day, I don't know what was going on in that place or in that neighborhood. When I go back, as I do on occasion, all seems normal. The old building still stands. The whore store is long gone. People come and go in the streets, all seems well, but I know that the secrets of our haunted world hide there still, even in the light of present days.

Such things have been with me all my life. I described many of my childhood experiences in *The Secret School*. And I wonder, now, if there aren't simply certain people who, perhaps because of shattering childhood trauma, see a little more of our world as it really is, at least at times.

The young man on Sulawesi who escaped the djinn was able to do so because he could see them, and there is in his story a very interesting hint of what might really be going on, and perhaps even the beginnings of an explanation of where we may be headed.

As they went deeper into the jungle and he saw more of the strange creatures who were following them, he also began to notice bizarre animals, large, antlered creatures. The world began to become different, and perhaps this is because it *was* different. Maybe there are worlds within worlds, and places where the barrier between them is, for whatever reason, thin.

Without realizing it, the young man and his friends had crossed a border. His friends disappeared into the other world altogether. Because he could see what was happening, even without understanding it, he was able to find his way back.

What subsequently happened to the ones who disappeared I have no idea, but I wouldn't be too surprised if they return one day, or some of them do, with no awareness of how much time has passed.

In my book *Breakthrough*, I recounted an experience of driving my car into what seemed to be another world. I was taking one of my son's friends from our cabin to Paramus, New Jersey, to meet his father.

I turned off the highway at the usual exit and, to my absolute amazement, found myself driving down a street in what looked like another world. I was completely stupefied. The boy was frightened, also, and began trying to get out of the car. I thought that I had veered into another universe, and had taken this poor child with me, perhaps never to return.

We drove along wide, shaded streets. Set back in deep yards were low structures looking nothing like normal houses.

Fortunately, we got back, only to find that what had seemed like a journey of about five minutes had actually consumed the better part of half an hour. But I will never forget those wide, silent streets and the strange buildings I saw set back among the trees looking like great blocks of stone carved with serpents.

It was not a place I would want to be. It was certainly not a place I would want to take a child.

There had been a sort of prequel to this event so bizarre that it seems beyond the pale even for a narrative like this. But it happened and so I will relate it as I remember it.   ·

I woke up in the middle of the night in bed, and found myself to be invisible. I had no body. It was so improbable that I would have laughed aloud—except, of course, I couldn't. After a moment, though, I came to full consciousness. I was simply an awareness in the vicinity of the bed. There was no "me."

A cold uneasiness went through me. Where was my body?

As soon as that thought materialized, I began to drift downward. In a moment, I was in the bedroom below ours, and there stood my body.

Both boys were wide awake and I was talking to my son's friend—or my body was.

Then I was inside myself and looking down at him. His expression, wide-eyed and interested, suggested that I was in mid-sentence. But what had I been saying? I had no idea. So I simply told them good night and went back upstairs.

As we were cooking breakfast the next morning, the boys' door burst open and they came running out, yelling, "Whitley came down through the ceiling last night." They had been awakened by a crackling sound, and down I had come, the physical part of me, pajamas and all.

It was just so extremely peculiar, I couldn't imagine what to make of it. How could a dream like that have any basis in reality? But it had, apparently. I asked the boys what we had been talking about, but they couldn't remember anything except me saying good night.

Later that morning, the adventure of slipping into the other world happened. Could some aspect of me that I am not in touch with have known what was going to happen, and was I instructing the boy about it?

The caterpillar will never understand the butterfly, I suppose, and perhaps what we are really looking at when we look at the close-encounter experience is an unsuspected transformation that is the fate of us all, into another state that is larger in scale than this one, and so very different that contact with ourselves in that condition seems like contact with aliens.

Nature is a cunning mistress and very, very old. Homo sapiens is something of a mystery, having leaped onto the scene just a few hundred thousand years ago. Perhaps we are even more of a mystery than we imagine . . . or than we *can* imagine.

Little did I know on that first night at the cabin what sort of adventures lay in store for me there. I felt uneasy, though, and felt more and more so in the coming months. I had bought the place expecting a refuge for my family from the noise and danger of the city, but by the time summer had rolled around, I was regularly drinking myself to sleep when we were there.

I would listen to the radio until late hours, drinking vodka and letting the music carry me through to the predawn, when I would sleep for a while, then wake up to bacon frying and laughing children and a wife in the middle of her life, a world of hope in her eyes and glory in the happy cries of the kids. So lovely and so normal. But something was *wrong*.

Just what it was is hard to articulate, but in that place, for me, the world was not unfolding in the patterns I had been taught to expect. But then again, in my life it never has, I suppose.

The cabin was on a community road, maintained privately, and all of us homeowners were responsible for our shares. A few months after my close encounter, our road needed spring maintenance, and one morning one of my fellow residents came over to discuss what was to be done.

While this was after the close-encounter experience it was before *Communion* was published, so he knew nothing about any of those things. However, the night before, we had heard a sound coming from deep under the cabin, like the high-pitched whine of some sort of drill. It was the kind of sound that made your teeth hurt.

The previous evening, also, I had seen somebody in the cabin, a boy of perhaps eleven, wearing a white T-shirt. He stared at me for a moment, then disappeared before my eyes.

In those days, I was also numb to the fear. I had become incurious about apparitions, frankly. My rule was: if I couldn't see it and touch it, maybe it was there and maybe not, but I just didn't give a damn.

Some very, very hard things happened in that first year after the close encounter, things that were too unbearable to write about. Suffice to say that at one point, the visitors had done something to me that is reported again and again in the accounts of close-encounter witnesses. They had put a baby in my arms. To this day, the sleeping face of this infant is burned into my soul, I can tell you, and in those days the memory was a raw, bleeding wound.

So I just ignored the damnable drilling sound when it started up again during our meeting. I didn't want to think about it, not any of it. Maybe they had some reason to be mining in the seam of iron that ran beneath the area—who knew?

When the sound began to get really penetrating, my neighbor became uncomfortable. He paused, then continued describing what he thought we needed to do to the roadbed.

The sound grew more intense.

The next thing I knew, a stream of blood came spurting out from between his eyes. It started spattering all over the room, and Anne came rushing up with Kleenex to staunch it.

He left and, understandably, never returned. Any further business we had, we did on the phone.

That afternoon, we went to another neighbor's house for more road discussions, taking our son and his playmate of the weekend with us.

Their house was in an uproar. They'd found a black dog on their deck, mysteriously dead, and their cat had disappeared.

In their house, I couldn't hear the drilling but I could feel it. I wondered if the death of the dog and the disappearance of the cat were somehow connected with it.

Our son's friend strolled into their living room, which had a lovely view. Suddenly, he whipped around with a horrified expression on his face. Blood was gushing out of both of his nostrils. Once again, we were frantically staunching bleeding. Anne called his mother, who corroborated his story that he'd never had another nosebleed in his life.

I'd had enough. We packed up and returned to the city. There was no way we were exposing those children to any more experiences like that.

The cat reappeared and the dog was autopsied, but no cause of death was ever found. If the two hunters in Brazil had also been autopsied, I wouldn't be surprised if the result would have been the same.

Black dogs have a long history in legend in Britain, in Latin America, and among UFO experiencers. The ghostly black dog called Black Shuck roams the Norfolk coastline, and in British folklore black dogs are associated with the land of the dead. In 1577, Black Shuck supposedly crashed through the doors of a church at Blythburgh, killed a man and a boy, and left scorch marks on the church doors.

Universally in European myth, black dogs have been associated with death and the world of the dead, Cerberus, the guardian of Hades, being the prime example.

When I saw the mysterious black dog lying on our neighbors' deck, I was aware of all this, but I didn't associate an ordinary-looking dead Lab with Cerberus. Perhaps I should have.

Two weeks later, we returned to the cabin. Anne and our son were happy there. What I was going through was hardly noticeable to them in those days. When I told Anne about my initial close encounter, she'd reacted with relief. She'd been trying to figure out why I was attempting to get her to leave our marriage. Now it was explained. I'd thought I was going insane, and I wanted her to take our boy and get far away from me.

My nights were one kind of hell and my days were another. I was compulsively walking out into the woods after midnight, even though I now knew that the visitors were real and I also knew that neither I nor anybody else had the slightest idea what they were.

Then another thing happened—small at the time, but part, I now believe, of the suggestive weave that this chapter is about. I believe it was that second week after the bloodlettings when our boy suddenly came out of his room and said, "Dad, there's a strange kid in the road."

I went out onto the porch and saw the child I had glimpsed before. He was on a black bicycle, standing there, looking at the house. He was pale, with black hair. He wore the most extraordinary shirt I had ever seen. It looked like some kind of armor, as if it was covered with knives.

As my son stood on the porch, I walked toward the boy. He got on the bike and rode off into a cul-de-sac behind our house. There was no outlet and the woods around it were thick enough to slow him down, although he could certainly have gotten through them. However, when I reached the road no more than half a minute later, he had entirely disappeared. Not quite before my eyes, but the next thing to it. Had he been aware that human attention fluctuates, and taken advantage of it? Is that how he disappeared?

We never saw him again, but I have to wonder if he did not come from the same place that all these other apparitions were from, a place that is closer to us in some ways than our own breath but is also not really here at all.

There is in physics a concept called alternative history. It has nothing to do with the usual speculations about Atlantis or whatever, but rather with what appears to be the truth about reality, that the universe is not a single, isolated entity at all but a component in a vast multiverse that includes parallel universes that are literal, physical places. Every possible outcome of every event happens somewhere, in what is probably an infinity of universes, forever expanding into a void that is without end.

It is a shocking idea, and when considered in the context of the coffin I was shown by the elderly visitor, it becomes an infinity from which there can be no escape: an unending, chokingly claustrophobic emptiness.

Some years ago, I read a paper by Oxford mathematician David Deutsch titled "The Structure of the Multiverse," which made this completely outrageous idea seem not only plausible but necessary to any sensible explanation of reality.

So could the existence of the multiverse be at least some of the reason for the bizarre effects associated with contact? Could there be some way to cross between parallel universes? But even if you could, you would not be real in any other universe you entered. You could not be. If so, then perhaps what we are looking at when we look at our visitors is, in our universe, essentially not real.

For us, perhaps the transformation into butterfly involves being recast in a parallel universe.

In this universe the whole anomalous enterprise may be an apparition being projected here by some sort of arcane technology or mental state that enables a crossing of the invisible gap between the worlds. So might they not indeed be us in another state?

Seemingly an arcane question, but is it? Truthfully we don't know, but with enough study, we could probably at least gain some focus on it.

If parallel universes are physically real and movement between them is possible, even if to only a limited extent, then a great deal that now makes no sense about the close-encounter experience would certainly come into focus.

A significant amount of the ambiguity in the experience, and some of the physical effects, such as creatures that can dematerialize, seem very hard to explain unless the laws of quantum physics sometimes apply at the classical level of reality. But surely arcane things like quantum indeterminacy don't apply to objects even as large as atoms. Only at the very smallest scale does the universe tolerate—and need—contradictions like things being both wave and particle at the same time.

Or so we used to think. In 2010, physicists Andrew Cleland and John Martinis of the University of California at Santa Barbara succeeded in causing a classically sized bit of metal to vibrate at two different rates at the same time. The magazine *Science* called it the most important discovery of the year, and said, "It opens up a variety of possibilities ranging from new experiments that meld quantum control over light, electrical currents and motion to, perhaps someday, tests of the bounds of quantum mechanics and our sense of reality."

I doubt if the author of that statement has any idea that the human mind seems already to be involved in quantum-physical reality. So much for the "quantum" in quantum physics. At least as far as my life is concerned, reality is already indeterminate. And I suspect that this is true for all of us. Just some of us, our boundaries shattered, see the truth. Our indeterminate, multilayered reality is not the illusion. The world of classical, linear mechanics is the illusion.

The fact that our visitors are often seen walking through walls, as I have personally seen, may not be technological legerdemain at all. It could be learned behavior. Perhaps they are able to control their movement in such a way that they can go into superposition and suddenly function as a wave rather than, as it were, a particle—as I may have done on that very odd night.

The Santa Barbara experiment shows that indeterminacy can apply to objects much larger than photons. The object placed in two states at once was tiny, but it contained trillions of atoms.

Given the speed with which science is evolving, in just a generation or two, we might well have complex machines that can be oscillating and standing still at the same time. Indeed, we might have a whole array of technologies that would look to us today like magic. People who change form and go through walls. The ability to transform into superposition with all the potentials for strange movement and limitless communication that this implies.

Maybe driving into other universes in a car isn't more than just imaginative misinterpretation of commonplace events. Maybe such things can actually happen. And maybe we all know it, but are in denial because we are here for reasons that have to do with living like caterpillars so that we can later live like butterflies.

Maybe, when we look at our visitors, we are looking at shepherds— who, to the sheep they control, appear to be more like jailers. Being nipped at by dogs and confined to tight herds cannot be pleasant for sheep. They might look hungrily at lush nearby pastures and wish their shepherds ill. But they do not see, perhaps, the shadow of the wolf there, nor understand the meaning of his call.

When we look at our visitors and their works, maybe we are looking at an evolution of ourselves and maybe not, but we are certainly looking at something that is much more deeply involved in our world than we have so far imagined.

Except . . . what if there's another side to this? Shepherds don't educate their sheep in the hidden meanings of their own lives. But our visitors are different. Once I got over my fear, I was admitted to what amounts to a school. When I began walking out into the woods at night in February of 1986, clutching a flashlight and so scared that I could hardly put one foot in front of the other, I did not realize it, but I was applying for admission to a school.

At the time, I was terrified and acting under what felt like a kind of compulsion. I did not understand that my abduction had really been an invitation, or, perhaps more accurately described, a dare.

I have been in this school now for many years, and in December of 2007, I had one of the most interesting lessons I've ever experienced.

I relate it now because it has to do with parallel universes and the possibility that they are not as isolated from one another as we now assume.

I'd long since lost the cabin. I was deep into the decade of research and reflection that would lead to this book.

I had just published a novel called *2012: The War for Souls*, which was a tongue-in-cheek exploration of parallel universes. In it, a meddlesome author gets himself into trouble by writing a novel that turns out to be a description of actual events unfolding in two parallel universes that occupy the same conditional space that ours does.

Immediately after I published the book, I happened to be looking at the *Daily Telegraph* online edition when I saw the following words in the September 27 edition: "Parallel universes really do exist, according to a mathematical discovery by Oxford scientists that sweeps away one of the key objections to the mind boggling and controversial idea."

It turned out that David Deutsch had published some more work that suggested not only that parallel universes are quite real but that they probably make time travel possible without such barriers as the grandfather paradox. This is because you wouldn't actually move through time. What would happen to the time traveler is that he would enter another universe that is unfolding on a different timeline.

Prior to the work of Erwin Schrödinger and Hugh Everett—in the days of John Von Neumann—it was believed that the wave function collapsed from the indeterminate state called superposition into what we see as reality.

However, the mathematics of this don't actually work very elegantly. There is mathematical elegance, however, in the notion that the collapse never actually takes place, but rather there is a process of continuous splitting—alternative histories—which effectively creates parallel universes.

But could they be real, living places, full of versions of ourselves, all with lives and pasts and aspirations? Could they have the vast material form that our own universe possesses? And how would the entities in them actually relate to us? Moreover, who would they be—us with just slightly altered pasts, or with radically different morphology—in effect, aliens who are, in some sense, us?

If parallel universes exist, well and good, but crossing the barrier between them seems even more impossible than traversing distances measured in light years. This is because, even if close ideations of us exist in parallel universes, we do not. It's not a matter of simply traveling there via some sort of science-fictional machine. The barrier is existence itself, and vague ideas of crossing it are the stuff of dreams.

Unless, of course, such dreams are real.

On the night of December 6, 2007, I found myself reading and rereading a passage in my book *The Key*, which I had published some years before. It is a transcript of a transcendent conversation with a man who had knocked on the door of my hotel room in the wee hours of the morning, whom I have come to call the Master of the Key. I turn to it often, reading its wisdom and wondering what on earth it really is.

I would like to say that it must have been a product of my imagination, and I am the Master of the Key. But the morning after I met him in 1998, I telephoned my wife and told her to never let me do this. I told her he had been entirely real. But we both knew of my tendency to want to believe that my strange experiences are explainable in whatever way seems most likely. Living in question, as I must do if I am going to approach any of this with integrity, is most uncomfortable.

The Master of the Key came into my life in quite an unexpected way. In June of 1998 I was asleep in my hotel room in Toronto, having just completed the last day of the author tour for *Confirmation*, the last nonfiction book I would write about strange realities for more than a decade.

There came a knock at the door, which I assumed was the room-service waiter. When I opened the door, an older man entered, walked across the room, and started talking. My initial reaction was to try to throw him out, but then he made an interesting and novel statement about the Holocaust, to the effect that a couple had died in it whose child would have discovered how to manipulate gravity.

I know very well that we're trapped on earth, and will be until we solve this precise problem. We're never going to get anywhere useful with rockets. To leave the planet in numbers, even to consider spreading into our own solar system, we need much more potent forces at our disposal.

So he had hooked me. Whoever he was, I started listening.

He made a number of scientific predictions, some of them quite outré. I recall how I laughed to myself when he commented, in regard to intelligent machines, that there were gases that could be made to store super-dense memory.

As I discussed in the introduction to the Tarcher/Penguin edition of *The Key*, this and other predictions of his have come true.

He also said that there were "many universes." At the time, there was not the slightest indication of this in scientific theory that I was able to uncover. Later, some astronomers theorized that a nine-billion-light-year gap in the universe might be caused by gravity from another one, so far away that its light has not yet reached us.

But then, in 2010, scientists at the University College in London found tentative evidence that our universe has collided with other universes four times in its history, with each collision leaving a signature in the background radiation.

Among the many magnificently interesting things this man said came in answer to my question, "Have you traveled to other worlds?" He replied, "I belong to many worlds."

I wondered at the time if this meant that parallel universes, a very different matter from other universes in this physical reality, might also be physically real.

I'm familiar with many-worlds theory, so his choice of that specific phrase resonated with me, and made me consider more carefully such experiences, admittedly more humble, and to be sure, funnier, as entering another world in my car, or having my body go off without me.

Could he have been saying that he was *conscious* in many parallel universes at the same time?

On the rainy night of December 6, I might have come into contact with an answer to that question.

I was sleeping my usual uneasy sleep when I was awakened by somebody clutching two fingers of my right hand. I came fully awake.

The idea entered my head that Anne had let a pack of feral dogs into the apartment, and they were under the bed.

I immediately got up to check the apartment. If the visitors were here, I wanted to meditate with them if possible. It had been a long time and it was really an experience to be treasured.

But when I stepped out into the living room, checking was hardly necessary. There were no visitors visible anywhere, but things were not in their usual order, not by any means. It wasn't even our apartment. There were four shrubs in it, in big square planters.

I immediately remembered the stories of what happened when people who went with the fairy folk touched things in their reality, or ate their food. They didn't return.

But when I turned around to go back to the bedroom, it seemed that I had already made the transition. The door wasn't there anymore. Instead, I was facing a wall, with a hallway leading off in the opposite direction.

Then I was in bed again, aware that I was asleep, but also that I was inside the consciousnesses of a number of different Whitleys at the same time. In different parallel universes? I felt that I was living all these lives at the same time.

Anne was in all but one of the lives. In it, I was walking along a quay with a small boy. Anne had died of the stroke she had in 2004, and the boy was my grandson.

In another reality, Anne and I were living in my old family home in San Antonio. We were poor. I had never left Texas and my life was a failure.

In a third, we were asleep in bed. Here, the "dogs" were under the bed. Here, somebody grabbed my fingers.

When I woke up, it was 4:53 by the clock that glows on Anne's bedside table. I could see lights in the sky outside the bedroom window. The wind was blowing hard, but the lights were absolutely still. Back in upstate New York, I'd sometimes seen such things, shapes and lights standing as still as stones amid storm clouds.

I leaped up, shouting to Anne that there was an object outside the window. I grabbed a camera I keep nearby, but when we got to the window, we couldn't see anything. So we went back to bed. When I put my head on the pillow, at just the right angle, I could see it again. Once more, I jumped up with the camera, but it turned out it was visible from only that one narrow angle. It was also moving now, and my last glimpse was of the thing going into the wind and out to sea—a not inappropriate direction, one might think.

So what happened this time? A close-encounter experience where I was "educated" in the reality of parallel universes? Yes. A vivid dream? Yes. So are the parallel universes I saw, then, real? Indeed, yes. Are they imaginary? Certainly.

From my experience, we are not living in a simple world where a table is a table and a chair is a chair. In the real world, the waveform never collapses because it can't collapse. Therefore, there is, quite simply, no such thing as the unreal. Everything is happening. An infinity of universes is spinning endlessly into an unfillable eternity, and consciousness flickers among them like static electricity, at once fluttering at random and seeking toward its destiny.

It's no wonder that our visitors appear to be as mad as hatters. Of course they're mad. We are going to go mad too, in the long run, but it will be, like theirs, an orderly madness. I suspect that a degree of insanity is essential to bearing reality as it actually is.

But, of course, we also won't go mad. In some aspects of our being, we will decline into nonmeaning. In others, we will find a way out of the labyrinth, and make new meaning for ourselves.

It is in this direction that I sought from the beginning to point my consciousness. And, as it turned out, I was not alone. I had help, as it were, from the other side.

CHAPTER 13
The Life of the Dead

WE ARE MORE THAN WE IMAGINE, A
fact that became vividly clear to me
one day in 1988 when I received a telephone call from my agent. He said that
there was a man trying desperately to reach me. He was an FAA inspector, and, in his desperation, he had investigated me deeply enough to
find my literary agent, no small feat in those days before the Internet.

I took his number and called him back.

He told me that a few nights before, he and his wife had been in
their living room at about ten when their elderly dog had suddenly
become nervous and needed to go out for a second time. His wife put
the dog on his leash, and as she opened the front door, she saw a fiery
ball of light speed low overhead and disappear behind the trees.

She called out that he would be getting an alert soon, because a
plane had just gone down in flames.

At that moment, their ten-year-old boy came running downstairs, shouting, "Mommy, Daddy, little blue men just brought Charlie into my room, and he said to tell you he was okay!"

They were absolutely floored, because this older son had died in an auto accident the week before.

The man said to me, "I want to know if this is true. I want to know if anything like this has ever happened to anybody else."

I thought back to my own encounter of a few years before. I had seen a dead friend with the visitors. My mind surveyed Anne's reports of the letters we had received, and in that moment, I realized something that had never occurred to me before. People frequently reported seeing dead friends and relatives with the visitors. So I said, "It's pretty common. It actually happened to me."

We spoke for a few more minutes, and then he rang off, planning to let his wife know what I had said. Anne had a chart on the wall in her office, and I saw that she had written, "This has something to do with the dead."

The UFO investigators, who are looking for aliens from another planet, certainly didn't want to hear anything like this. By contrast, the skeptics would be eager to know more, because they would think that it would make the testimony seem even more absurd.

At least in this section of the book, I won't be inveigling for research, largely because I have no idea how that might be done. I am sure, though, that in the end it *will* be done, but first neuroscience has to find its way past its present endeavor, which is to determine how, and prove that, consciousness is an effect of brain function, not its cause.

In the end, though, the quest to deconstruct consciousness by determining the mechanisms by which the brain allegedly produces it will fail, just as things like the theory of the luminous ether have failed in the past. But it will take time. When, in 1884, the Michelson-Morley experiment, which was designed to quantify the speed of the earth against the background of the ether, failed, it should have been obvious that the ether, therefore, didn't exist. Instead, efforts began to be made to fix the theory.

It took the brilliant logic of Albert Einstein and his concept of special relativity in 1905 to finally reveal that the ether was just hot air, and it will take many failures before neuroscience exhausts the theory that consciousness is a brain function.

When that happens, it will be because somebody detects what I suspect is probably the reality: there is a level of conscious being that is an energetic field of some sort. It's not supernatural, and can exist outside of the body. In fact, that's its primary realm. But it is also not easily detectable, first because it's not being sought, and second because it probably controls the degree to which it can be known by us in the very physically invested state that we are in, encased in dense bodies that effectively enforce upon us an inability to perceive much of anything that isn't moving, like our bodies, through linear time.

In the years that followed my conversation with the FAA inspector, I began to see, more and more, that the dead were involved with our supposed alien visitors, and through them with us.

A typical example of this relationship unfolded at our cabin later in 1988. We had assembled a group with the intention of attracting the interest of the visitors, which had worked well in the past.

There were four people sleeping in the living room, and two in the basement beneath them. Nobody, naturally enough, was asleep. Some time after midnight, one of the people in the living room noticed that he was not able to move. He could talk, though, and he asked the others if they could move. Nobody could, but they could all talk and see.

What they saw was what appeared to them to be a troop of dwarf acrobats in dark blue clothes leaping around the room, a display that continued for five or ten minutes. When it ended and the little figures disappeared, the group was able to move again. They sat up, talking about what happened.

Nobody attempted to communicate with the couple in the basement, but it developed the next morning that they, also, had had an unusual experience. At about the same time, they had seen a friend of theirs standing at the foot of the bed. She seemed perfectly whole and normal, which was odd because she had been killed in the Mexico City earthquake of 1983. She told them that she was "all right."

So while the little blue figures—the sinister clowns seen by the psychologist and the "little blue men" observed by the FAA inspector's son and by Lorie Barnes—displayed themselves upstairs, a dead person showed up downstairs, looking perfectly well and completely whole.

I am reminded of Lorie's report that one of the creatures touched her hand and said, "One day, my dear, you will look just like us."

Are we looking, here, through the door that may have so distressed Dr. Von Neumann, and finding on the other side not aliens but another evolution of the human species, one that is wildly different from us but still very much a part of nature? Not exactly denizens of a parallel universe, but certainly butterflies to our caterpillars.

It seems to me that the persistent appearance of the dead in the company of the visitors suggests that their mere presence breaks down the most fundamental of all barriers, which is the one that separates the living from the dead.

The Master of the Key spoke of the existence of conscious energy and of people who become radiant beings, entirely composed of this energy. Of course I asked him how this worked. Were they plasmas or what?

If they are plasmas, then I would assume that they can be detected. On September 12, 2000, I was at the home of a man who had been photographing what people call "orbs." Now, I have to be frank about these things. I assumed that they were bits of dust or moisture that had confused the light sensors of digital cameras. Few orbs were photographed during the era of film cameras.

That night, however, I was standing in this man's backyard when I suddenly felt the strong presence of my mother, who died in 1994. It was a delightful moment, and a powerful one. She seemed to be just overhead, and about ten feet in front of me. The sense of presence was really amazing, so strong that I wanted to hold her in my arms.

At that moment, somebody took a picture of me. In it, there is a distinct spark of light just where I was sensing the presence. The expression on my face communicates the pleasure and intensity of the experience, and my face is turned directly toward the spark. The photograph is available on unknowncountry.com.

I wonder if a part of the close-encounter experience might be to break down the barrier between physical humanity and radiant humanity? If so, then the physical brain is challenging its encasement in space-time with another evolutionary development: it is becoming able to see this other form of human life, and to communicate with it and learn from it.

Long before my encounter with my mother, I'd spent the most extraordinary years of my whole experience in contact with a truly amazing person, who could straddle the line between the world of physical man and that of radiant man.

Since 1970, I had been meditating nightly, and I had a meditation room included in the new cabin that we'd built in early 1989. In it, I would generally meditate for half an hour to an hour at around eleven o'clock every night.

I was there one night in the winter of 1990, when I heard movement behind me. I thought one of the cats had come in, but there was no cat there. I continued meditating but soon felt a need to turn around again. I could hear small sounds. Someone was behind me.

This time, I got up and turned on the light. The room was completely empty. So I turned it off and started again. As I was directing my attention to my body, I felt a distinct burst of air move past me. Again, I got up, this time to close the door.

For a while, all was quiet. But I couldn't shake the feeling that somebody was in the room. But how could there be? It wasn't a large room. It was clearly empty.

Finally, I had to quit. Deciding that my imagination had gotten the better of me, I stood up, saying aloud as I did so, "All right, if you're going to meditate with me, I'm going to have to see you."

With that, I went to bed, soon dropping into restless sleep, guns at the ready, light switches close to hand, camera on my bedside table. Since the previous spring when the implant had been put in my ear, I had been even more restless than usual.

On this night, I slept only intermittently. Somebody was moving around in the room, but when I opened my eyes, Anne was in bed. One cat was under the covers, the other asleep on the foot of the bed.

Finally, I got to sleep, but what seemed like only a few minutes later, I was waked up again by the sound of a cat jumping off the bed.

What I saw when I opened my eyes shocked me to my core. Sitting at the foot of the bed, his back against the footboard, was a man. He was perfectly distinguishable in the light from the glowing alarm-system console beside the bed.

He wore a light-colored tunic cinched at the waist by a dark belt. His eyes were deep and dark. I could feel them watching me. But there was no sense of menace. It didn't even cross my mind to go for the gun. Unfortunately, the same went for the camera. In the face of this amazing apparition, all of my plans slipped out of my mind. I cared about only one thing: I wanted to get closer to this man, to talk to him, to touch him.

I drew myself out from under the quilt and slid down to the foot of the bed. I was now just a couple of feet from him. I could see him clearly. He had a middle-aged face, a narrow jaw, and slightly sunken cheeks. His eyes were normal in shape, but they were dark pools, as if sunken deeply into his head.

I looked at him closely. He was as still as a rag doll, his hands lying along the bed beside him. My guess was that he was under five feet tall, but a normally mature male.

I took one of his hands. It was light but entirely solid. I looked down at it resting in my hand. It was an adult hand but the size of a child's. There were no rings. Again I looked up at him. His lips were slack, but his eyes were definitely alive. This close, I could see the pupils gleaming in their depths.

There was a distinct ripeness about him, frankly. This was not a man who bathed very much, that was clear. I squeezed his hand, then lifted it and smelled his skin. The human odor was very strong.

"Who are you?" I asked.

No reply. I decided that I would turn on the lights, so I slid back up the bed and reached for the switch.

When it was on, he looked entirely human. Still, though, he hadn't moved. I looked at his clothing. His tunic was frayed along the shoulders. It was dirty. It was cinched with a cloth belt. This man not only smelled like a souk on a hot afternoon, he was dressed in rags.

Understand, at this point, probably under a minute had passed. I turned to Anne to wake her up. As I shook her, I remembered the camera. Lurching, I lunged for it.

The man was gone. Just like that. Anne, stirring from the movement in the bed, turned over and cuddled deeper into the quilt. From under the covers, our Siamese cat Coe continued to purr softly.

Camera in hand, I got up and searched the house. I never felt particularly threatened by this man, and didn't take a gun with me. Perhaps it was because he was so slight. In any case, it didn't occur to me. I turned on the outside lights and looked out the windows. I went into the basement, then up into the attic and turned on all the lights in both places.

There was nobody in the house. Our other cat, Sadie, was sleeping close to the fireplace, which still glowed with residual warmth. All was at peace.

I went back to bed and lay there, thinking about what had happened. First, I had sensed this man in the meditation room. Or sensed something. I'd said that I wouldn't meditate with him unless he showed himself, and lo and behold, a few hours later, he did.

Finally, I fell asleep. It seemed as if I'd been sleeping for about ten minutes when suddenly somebody started jabbing my shoulder. I woke up to see the man dashing off across the floor, heading in the direction of the meditation room.

Incredible.

It was actually about six, still more than an hour to winter dawn. I followed him. The room now appeared to be empty, but I settled down on the floor to meditate anyway. I was excited. It had been a couple of years since any physical contact had occurred, and never before with anybody so human in appearance.

I disciplined myself to meditate, releasing my breath, taking my attention to the sensation of my body, letting my mind go blank.

And nothing whatsoever happened. It felt as if there was nobody there but me. It was also cold and I was still sleepy. I gave it about fifteen minutes and then went back to bed.

I was frustrated, and in a way I had been many times before. There would be a dramatic buildup, then nothing. But not always. Sometimes the payoff had been incredible.

I kept to my 11 p.m. meditation schedule. From my previous encounters, I had already understood that meditation is also communication. The reason that I'd been able to deepen my relationship with the visitors was meditation.

Two or three more days passed with no response. We went about our lives.

Then it happened, a truly remarkable event. The meditation room had a cathedral ceiling, above which was the roof, and there came through that ceiling a number of loud, distinct thuds.

I sat wondering if what had just happened overhead involved my new visitor or, perhaps, raccoons or opossums? So I tried tapping three times on the floor where I was sitting.

Incredibly, awesomely, three taps were immediately returned from overhead.

Was it the man I had just met? More than one of them? I didn't know. But I did know one thing: this time, I was absolutely *not* going to run.

I'd not yet heard the frightening rumors about bizarre murders in nearby cities. I wonder, if I had heard them, whether or not I would have stayed in that room—or even kept the cabin any longer, for that matter. We were exposed there, totally exposed. I'd often gone a mile and more back into the woods and down into a cave in order to be alone with the visitors.

Now, they—or someone—had come to me. I worked to do better this time. I struggled to draw my mind away from thoughts like *They're here! They're meditating with* me*!*

After all, what if opossums had dropped down onto the roof, and I was meditating with them? While animals have a relationship to the sacred, we don't know what it is, and let's face it, nobody really knows how to meditate with them. In any case, opossums snort too much.

Then I realized that something was happening, something quite new. My mind was sort of *moving*. I was seeing pictures from my own past. It wasn't as dramatic as I imagine the life review at the time of death might be, but these images kept appearing, one after the other.

It was exactly as if I was looking at an illustrated book of my memories. But it wasn't me doing this. Somebody else seemed to be turning the pages of my memory.

At first, the imagery was trivial. A childhood moment watching a neighbor's dog barking at our cat under a tree. Another skating at night in our driveway. As a teenager, sitting on the back porch with my first girlfriend, listening to taps sound from nearby Fort Sam Houston.

Then it became more complex, with images from related experiences superimposing themselves on one another. Looking back, I cannot even begin to describe them all. There were hundreds, thousands. But at the time, this didn't seem in the least difficult to follow. What was fascinating was all this detail. Where was it coming from? I couldn't have even begun to call these memories up at will, and yet when I saw each one, it was achingly familiar.

How lovely it was. How delicious my life had been, how beautiful— and how much of it I had let pass by!

The little, tiny things that we forget the moment they happen—the scent of the evening, the tremble in a voice, the fluttering of leaves, a squirrel scolding as I walked to a car—these sorts of memories are what I was experiencing, and I found myself loving life in a completely new way, knowing that it is not the great memories only that confer meaning on it but also the small things, the tiny ones, which are left like diamonds in the mine of the past, upon which personality and ego float like an ephemeral foam. And yet we live in this ephemera. It's where we engage with what of life we imagine is important.

And then, suddenly, I was focused on something very specific. It was the face of a woman. I knew it well. It was a woman I had wanted. Badly. And she had wanted me. We'd come close to connecting in a way that would have violated my marriage vow. I had really sweated over this. I had wanted her so badly. But I had not quite let myself slip into a love affair. Not quite.

But what was it that had stopped me, my loyalty to my vow or my love of my wife? A man might love his wife, but a temptation like this can be very powerful, and it certainly had been for me.

Then the memories ended. I slumped to the floor, devastated. I was pouring with sweat. Shocked and confused and telling myself, *You weren't* disloyal. *You resisted the temptation.*

I did not want to face what I had *not* resisted, which was the desire. I had been the instigator. My challenge to my vow and to the selfless love my wife has given me since the day we met was my doing. I had not been seduced, and that was very hard to face.

I got the hell out of that meditation room. What was going on? I just wanted to forget what I had done. Nobody likes to face a truth like that.

I went into the bedroom. There Anne lay, sound asleep. I was disgusted with myself. She'd given everything to our marriage. So had I held something back? Who did I think I was, anyway, not to give as much as she had?

But then I saw the woman's face again, this time in the dimness of normal memory, and I was stirred again by the heat in her eyes, the clearly expressed longing. If only I had taken the relationship one more step, then I would have known her. Before I met my wife, I had made love only once, so I have always been curious about other women. But I made a vow to her before God, and I would never dream of breaking it. In any case, she is a joyously satisfying partner for me.

Still, I went to bed feeling bitter and confused and unsure of my loyalties. Only gradually did sleep come, and it was a fitful sleep.

Then I was awake. And what I was seeing was completely beyond the pale. Completely incredible but so totally real that it never even entered my mind in the moment that it was in any way an illusion.

When I had opened my eyes, at first what I was seeing simply didn't make sense. There were two large objects on the ceiling above the bed. Then I realized what they were, and I almost fainted, such was the terror that shot through me.

What I was looking at were two enormous spiders hanging on the ceiling. And I don't mean, for example, the size of tarantulas. These things were tremendous. Their abdomens were at least three feet long, gleaming black and banded by yellow tiger stripes. And what was worse, while the one over my side of the bed seemed stable, the one hanging over Anne was struggling and looked as if it was about to fall on her.

Instinct caused me to leap out of the bed, and as I did so, I thought that this was one hell of a nightmare.

I stood there just absolutely agog, because the things had not disappeared when I woke up. They still looked completely real. And there was a scratching sound, getting louder.

The one hanging over Anne was trembling now. It was starting to fall. There were clicks and louder scratching sounds. Three of its legs were out of contact with the ceiling.

She lay on her back, sound asleep, her face in repose, her body communicating innocent and total trust.

I could run, and my instinct was to do just that. I could call to her, but what would happen then? She'd panic and the thing was likely to fall. Or I could go over there and lean over her and shield her with my body.

In that moment, a deep truth came boiling up from within me. She was so precious to me that there was not the slightest question: if I had to, I was going to give my life for her.

I did not know what they were. I did not know where they had come from. But I no longer lived in the expected world. In my world, this new world, anything could happen.

As quietly as I could, I moved around the bed. I slid in beside her. She sighed and smiled, welcoming her husband. I slipped over her and held her to me, and lay like that, afraid to move. The core of my heart seemed to open, and I remembered why I loved this woman, and knew the value of the years she had given me, the value of her heart, and reconnected with the love that has been my home since first I kissed her.

I was left like that. At some point, the spiders of nightmare had gone.

What had happened to me was completely typical of the way I

now lived. A richly evocative, extremely complex dream had come that was also a communication, and, in a way we do not yet have the language to describe, a real experience.

What a gift I had been given. The truth of the great love of my life had been restored to me, but it had come with a warning. I must have the courage to nurture it, and I must treat it, and Anne, with the respect that is deserved.

My marriage, which I had not even realized I was challenging, had been saved, from my own selfishness and blindness.

The message was very clear, and this was the beginning of what has become the moral journey of my life. Purity and dedication are essential. Love is not passion, and love matters. It is what we have that is real, and what we take with us when we leave the body.

As I soon discovered, we go on quite a journey. Yes, it takes place entirely in the physical world. But we know only a very small corner of that world, those of us who are living this life. One day, we will take our experiences with us into another state of being. The lives we have lived will be our clothing—what the Bible calls the coat of many colors.

I was given a tremendous gift on that night. It was a simple but clear instruction about what is worth taking with us when we go on, and what is not.

CHAPTER 14
The Master of the Key

MY WIFE HAS GIVEN EVERYTHING SHE has to our marriage. She didn't necessarily want to. I am quite sure she would have been very glad if the close encounter had never happened and, above all, if I had never written *Communion*. By the time the nineties came along, she had seen most of her friends in New York walk away from her. She had seen her position as the wife of a prominent author and an intellectual in her own right turned into a mockery.

She was bitter and tired, and yet not a day passed that she did not work on the letters, which, three years after *Communion* was published, were still pouring in. She would sit reading and making notes, filing and, often, answering them or calling people who seemed to be especially in need.

I was miserable too, of course, and she never wavered for a moment in her support. From the moment I'd told her what happened, she had been on my side without question. Her faith in me was total. But she was also a persistent and careful skeptic, but one of the members of the skeptical religion like I had been, whose skepticism was really just another insupportable belief. Anne was a genuine skeptic, seeking always to find the right questions and, above all, to articulate them correctly. Her skepticism was founded in an intellectual commitment to the truth, not in the arrogance that animates the organized community of skeptics.

She was also, as she always had been, a lovely and desirable woman, a truly good woman, who had given me a son, the only male heir in my family, and he was a fine, strong, and intelligent child.

This was Anne as she was then. On my side, despite my moment of temptation, I had always been utterly and willingly loyal. She is such a dynamic, captivating woman, how could I be anything else? That I was even tempted has troubled me for years, despite the fact that I know how male instinct works, and that such temptations are natural.

And now I'd had a really extraordinary intervention into my marriage by somebody who obviously cared about her, cared about both of us, and had taken me through one of the most powerful and transformative experiences of my life, which had guided me back to the feelings that are at the foundation of my marriage, and had reminded me of just how essential they are to me and to us.

I was in a new and much different situation from ever before. I had met a man who looked very human but had really remarkable abilities. He could disappear at will. And yet he could also be entirely material. He could do things to my mind that I had never imagined possible. The illusion of the spiders had really been stunning—if it was an illusion.

Those thuds on the roof, though—they had been real. So the next afternoon, I went up on the roof in an effort to see if there was any possibility that animals could have dropped down out of the trees the night before. But there were no trees overhanging the roof. When I looked up, all I saw was what I knew I would see: the sky.

It was a lonely and strange moment. I went back down, and I spent the afternoon sitting in my office, wondering what had happened. Later, I heard Anne downstairs singing, and her voice seemed to carry a new tone, almost a secret lilt. I thought to myself: *She knows. She knows it all. The temptation, the test, the outcome. And she's happy. She knows that her marriage is strong.*

I assumed that this was the beginning, middle, and end of the experience. Another remarkable, inexplicable journey to the shadow-line between reality and dream, punctuated by a wonderful, renewing intervention on behalf of a great marriage and a woman of excellence.

The evening passed, our son went to bed, Anne went to bed, and silence settled.

Eleven o'clock came and I went to my meditation room, followed by the cats. I had not been sitting for three minutes when there was a series of thuds on the roof. The cats rushed out of the room immediately.

I sat stunned, trying to face the facts: these people were *real*. They were also much less shy than the little gray creatures who had been in my life before. For one thing, they seemed to know me a lot better. I had never had an experience with the grays that was remotely as connected to my life as last night's had been.

I tapped three times on the floor. Immediately, there came back three taps from above.

This was an unusual experience, to say the least, and I can assure you that it is just as amazing as it sounds. There is no elegant way to dismiss it as an illusion or some sort of "imaginal" experience. It was real. I was entering into yet another relationship of a new kind.

Unlike what it had been like when I was going out into the woods, there was not the slightest sense of menace. I felt as if these were people. I sensed that they understood me. I knew, also, that they were on the side of my marriage and of Anne, and therefore on my side.

I waited, expecting I don't know what. But nothing seemed to happen. We simply meditated together. After half an hour, I went to bed.

At three in the morning, I was awakened by somebody jabbing at my shoulder. When I opened my eyes, a small man was standing at the bedside, looking down at me with dark, shadowed eyes.

The moment I moved, he dashed away, completely disappearing as he ran across the bedroom toward the hall that led to the meditation room.

I followed, and meditated again for about twenty minutes. I was expecting, at the very least, to have the secret of life revealed to me. But nothing unusual happened.

At six, the same process was repeated, and the next night and the next. Night after night, I slept only in short bursts. I went into a period of intensive meditation with them that lasted until we returned to Manhattan in the fall. For the next few months, though, whenever we were at the cabin, they were there.

My marriage became more intimate than it had ever been. Also, though, our money troubles increased. The rejection of me in the media was total now. I had not delivered what the public wanted, which was proof that aliens were real and were here, so I was at this point generally considered a liar. If I wasn't being accused or ridiculed, I was being tuned out. At the time, I was writing *Breakthrough* and hoping that it would somehow save my career. In it, I told many of the extraordinary stories of what had happened to us. I was able to name some of the witnesses.

None of it mattered.

We should never have built our expensive new cabin, and Anne hadn't wanted to, but I was eager to preserve the land that the visitors were appearing in, and had bought a hundred and fifty acres and put it under a perpetual conservation easement. Also, there had been trouble at the old cabin. One of my neighbors had told me that he had seen lights appearing above it at times, and heard a sort of mournful sound, and this story had filtered through the community. Another neighbor was fairly sure that he had seen the close encounter that led to *Communion*, and had apparently spoken about this around town.

He and his wife had been coming home from a party at around 2:30 on the morning that it happened, and had seen what they thought was a blimp down in a field about a mile from our houses. He had gotten out to see if anybody was hurt. When he heard screaming, he began to run toward the thing. Suddenly lights appeared all over it, and it began moving in his direction. In the car, his wife panicked. So did he, for that matter. He raced back to the car and, with the thing hanging over the field nearby, they left the area.

As rumors spread, people began driving past the cabin. Once, a man went past showing a shotgun. People would come up and bang on the door in the middle of the night. The stone circle where the encounter had taken place attracted more and more vandalism.

I felt that the old cabin was too exposed, which was my motive for wanting to move. But the new place had cost too much. I had depleted my finances even as my book sales were collapsing.

When the summer of 1991 came, we moved up to the cabin full-time. We could no longer afford two residences. After a few nights, I once again heard the thudding on the roof.

Night after night, the pattern was repeated. I would enter the meditation room, the sounds would come, I would meditate. Usually, I was entirely within myself—at least, as much as one ever is during meditation—but every so often there would be a sort of communication, but so fleeting and subtle that I cannot with truth say exactly what might have been meant.

Still, the meditation was wonderful. I began to feel an incredible physical lightness and an inner joy. But my life continued to collapse, and more and more frequently, the joy would implode into despair. How could I lose this? What would happen after? If we had to leave, would the experience follow us?

As she cataloged our letters, Anne was assembling a larger and larger collection of extraordinary human experience. She would bristle when she would hear supposed authorities on television explaining that these were all people with "fantasy-prone personalities," attention-seeking liars, or people looking for money, or that close encounters were sleep disturbances.

Then night would come, and with it another peak experience of direct contact with unknown beings.

One night, Anne said that she had decided that she was going to meditate with me. I was overjoyed. I'd been wanting this from the beginning. Anne took all of the hard knocks and worked entirely in the background, and not only that, had absolutely no contact.

She came in with me and sat down. In a few minutes, my friends came banging down on the roof as always. I was delighted. I said, "They're here. That's them."

For a moment, she sat as still as a deer. I thought to myself that she was afraid, but I didn't get a chance to reassure her. She said, "I'm not ready for this," and got up and left.

She never came back, but she also never flagged in her work, as she never has, not in all these years. People may doubt the close-encounter witnesses, twist their stories to make them appear to be things that they are not, lie to them and about them, persecute them and dismiss them, but not Anne. She has read too many letters and seen too much. She knows.

I found it quite frustrating that I would have these amazing beings showing up at night but be unable to communicate with them beyond simply sitting in silence together, and unable to prove their existence.

One night, I set up a video camera aimed at the roof, to try to record some sort of video of their arrival. That night, they didn't come.

In fact, whenever I set up the camera, they didn't come. But when it wasn't there, they did. Fearing that I would drive them away altogether, I quit trying.

Nothing changed with the meditations. Night after night, it was the same. Finally, I began trying to get them to tell me who they were. I had seen them materialize and dematerialize. I had experienced them doing extraordinary things with my mind. But who were they?

One night, a thought came into my mind. Or, rather, a word. It was "bardo." This was the Tibetan word for the world between lives. The next day, I found a book pulled out of a shelf in my basement library. It was called *Life Between Life*, by Dr. Joel Whitton and Joe Fisher. I'd had it for years but never really looked through it. Now I did, and found that it contained thirty of Whitton's case studies of people who remembered being in the bardo.

Now, at this time, I had been out of my body once—I mean, completely and cleanly. This had happened in early 1987, while I was still writing *Communion*. I'd been trying a method provided in Robert Monroe's book *Journeys out of the Body,* and had come out quite cleanly. I'd moved across the room, had looked back at our bed with my body lying in it, then moved out through the window and part of the wall into the front yard, where I'd seen all the trees covered with a shimmering electric field of some sort. I'd touched some pine needles but had been unable to pull them off.

I'd thought that it would be easy for me to leave my body again but, in fact, have never since done it that cleanly and clearly.

I went to a Gateway week at the Monroe Institute and gave Robert Monroe a galley proof of *Communion*. He said, "You'd better really want to do this, because it's going to cause you a lot of trouble." I had no idea what he meant. He said, "The U.S. government is going to just hate your book."

I thought he was a bit of a paranoid and dismissed the comment.

I could not dismiss what happened during the Gateway, though. A friend of mine, Bernard Hurwood, lay mortally ill in New York, and I had hesitated to leave because I wanted to be at his bedside if things took a turn for the worse.

To my amazement, he showed up during the Gateway in a sort of disembodied form. He looked like he was gliding. Time after time, I would see him out of the corner of my eye. But he wasn't at the Gateway, he couldn't be.

I telephoned his wife, and she said that he was very bad indeed. All week, I began to see him more and more clearly. Finally, I saw him sitting beside me in a lecture that Mr. Monroe gave, describing various levels of reality beyond the physical. He was listening intently.

Only after the lecture did it hit me yet again that he could *not* be there. When I got home, the first thing Anne said was, "Bernie died."

We used to have some fine times together, and I miss him to this day.

At this point, profound questions burned in me. What are human beings? Who are our visitors, really? Anne and I discussed these matters by the hour. We decided that the message was that there is a soul that can exist outside the body, but the life of the soul is a total and complete unknown. Our religions are little more than guesswork.

In August of 1994, we ceased to be able to pay our mortgage unless we stopped paying Andrew's school bills and my mother's rent. She had cancer and we obviously could not see her turned out.

On October 3, she died. The bank was pressing us. By the end of the month, our course of action was clear. We would have to leave the beautiful new cabin behind, leave everything, and move back to Texas. We'd have to occupy the little apartment where my mother had been living.

Even through all of this, the meditations got more and more intense.

In August, another element had been added, an appalling one. In July, I had received the telephone call warning me that some of the locals were planning for me to be the victim of a seeming hunting accident that fall. I told nobody about this, but we'd also found some evidence of sabotage around the house, so it was clear that our time here had come to an end.

Every night, though, I went into the meditation room and the same thing happened. Sometimes, although not often, I would feel hands on my shoulders. Once, on my cheek, and it was really very comforting.

The last night came. I went into the mediation room. For months, I had been begging them for help. The only reaction it would elicit would be uneasy shuffling on the roof.

I made a last request. This was the end of my time here. I would never return. Would they please show themselves again? I wanted to know their final reality. What did they actually look like?

I waited, but nothing happened. I said aloud, "Well, that's it. Good-bye." I went to bed and lay there in frank tears. Anne slept softly beside me. She was losing so much, most of her beautiful furniture, our library, many of her collections. She had already lost her beloved New York, and now the rest of it was going too. What had I done to this poor woman? If I loved her, why had I taken her in this direction?

I was lying there, commiserating with myself, when suddenly I saw a glow coming in the front windows of our bedroom. I thought the house had been set alight. During the summer, we had found a gasoline can mysteriously standing open beside our boiler in the basement. If the fumes had ignited, the house would have burned down, and us in it, probably, as we would have been asleep upstairs.

I rushed to the window and saw one of the most beautiful things I have ever witnessed. An enormous ball of light floated majestically away from the house and out over the front lawn. Emanating from it were hundreds of narrow shafts of light, and when they touched my skin I could feel them pricking me, and along with this sensation an absolutely shocking sense of intimacy with another person.

This *was* another person, in fact. I knew it at once. This was the person I had been meditating with all these years. He wasn't some great master, I don't think, no Christ or Buddha. Far from it, he felt familiar and ordinary. He felt like an ordinary person.

I was overawed, though. I felt reasonably sure that I had seen beyond the boundaries of this life, and what I had seen implied the existence of human beings in very different states from the physical.

From what I have seen, I suspect that our ideas of the afterlife are largely imaginary, but that it actually does exist.

From the day I began with the visitors in 1985 until this day nearly ten years later, I had learned so much. Certainly, I had been in a school. I'd known that almost from the beginning. But now the amazing purpose of this school was clear: it was to draw back the veil that stands between us and the world around us, and in so doing draw back the veil between the living and the dead.

On that night, I saw a dead man in his true state, shining with a living light. It was the most moving and most humbling experience I had ever had. And what was most remarkable was that despite the glory of his being, shining like a small sun, my impression was that I was in the presence of somebody who was humble, not a grand actor on a great cosmic stage.

I can't emphasize this enough: he was, to my mind, what ordinary people—good people—become. This caterpillar had a glimpse of the butterfly.

Then, in 1998, came the Master of the Key, and the little book that records my conversation with him.

I don't know where he came from or where he went, but I do know this: he presented me not only with some surprising scientific insights but also with ethical ideas of extreme clarity, and with what might be some directional ideas about what the soul actually is.

My meeting with him was the third fundamental experience of my life. The first was the 1985 close encounter, the second was the last night at the cabin. My meeting with him was the third, and perhaps the last.

The Master of the Key opened a door for me when he commented, "You must understand that the living and the dead share the same world." He then added, "You the living are changing now. As this change proceeds, you are better and better able to feel the presence of your dead."

I think that this is what has happened to me. I think that it explains my life. Not that everything I have seen and all the forms I have encountered are really our own dead, but that the entire enterprise of close encounter is about the dropping of the veil between those who are in physical form and those who the Master said are in "radiant" form.

I think the basic reason that the coming of the UFO is resisted so profoundly, and the close-encounter experience rejected, is that the extremely high levels of strangeness that accompany them create a frightful impression of chaos. The crop formations are glorious but frighteningly enigmatic. And the implants, what can they mean? And why in the world won't the "aliens" simply land and have done with it? It all comes down for most of us, in the end, to a strange and annoying nonsense that we choose to ignore.

But we ignore it in the same way that the mockingbird ignores the fact that he is clutching a telephone line full of conversations while he sings in the summer afternoon. He has no idea where he really is. His reality is not the whole world, but there is a difference between him and us. If we do not remain passive, and instead open our minds, we can begin to sense the vibrations, hear the conversations, later understand them, later still find our own music and come even to understand our true place as a part of mankind, but not all of mankind.

The Master said, "The science of the soul is just another science. There is no supernatural, only physics."

This enormous event that has been gradually coming into focus over the last century is encounter both with ourselves as other and with another consciousness. It is unfolding at the level of the soul, to which we are almost entirely blind, and I suspect that those of us in the physical are in the position of a two-dimensional being watching an orb pass through his plane. All we can see is a line that mysteriously expands, then contracts.

So of course most of what is transpiring remains enigmatic to us. It's not for us, no more than the music the shepherd is playing to pass the time is for the sheep. The music of close encounter, on our level, sounds dissonant and appears to have no consistent rules. UFOs come and go, or maybe it's all an illusion. Fantastic secrets are kept by government, or perhaps not. Crop formations speak, but in what language, and to whom? And all the while, the implants broadcast their fragile signals into the void—for perhaps twenty feet.

If contact between mankind and this other level of consciousness is not even happening primarily in what we think of as the physical world, but in another aspect of reality, then it might appear as it does to us: extraordinarily confusing.

Even so, there may be method behind the madness. There is only one way in which all of this makes sense at our level of being. If its purpose is to induce question in many and cause trauma in some, then it makes sense.

If so, then, at our level, it is operating as an attempt to shock us into a new kind of awareness. My speculation in *Communion* that what is happening to us might be what the force of evolution looks like when it is applied to a conscious mind would be essentially correct. Except that the force of evolution here would not be some vague urgency of nature but rather the combined efforts of our visitors and our own kind, operating together, but not, for the most part, in a partnership that extends into the physical world.

But what form would the shock take? I think that it's possible to speculate about that in a reasonably precise way.

CHAPTER 15
The Power of the Question

A FTER MY 1985 CLOSE ENCOUNTER, I HAD A galloping case of post-traumatic stress disorder (PTSD). Unfortunately, the various treatments I have tried have failed, probably because the stressor—the encounter experience—could always happen again at any moment. Thus, to this day I have terrific nightmares and wake up at the approximate time the encounter happened, usually with my heart hammering, waves of fear coursing through me.

Among other things, some sufferers of PTSD can experience flashbacks and hallucinations that seem real. They are thrown off the road of the real, and exist instead in an awful twilight of memories and illusions, and have no way to tell the difference between them.

I have lived like this for a long time. In fact, though, it is further support of the reality of my experiences. If nothing had happened to me, I wouldn't suffer from PTSD. You don't get it from bad dreams.

It has been found by psychologists in the UK seeking to find a mechanism that will predict which trauma sufferers will get PTSD that people who are already victims of it process information much more with the right hemisphere of their brain. This is what makes them experience flashbacks.

If you actually *wanted* people to increase the use of the right brain, then stressing them would be a way to do it. But it wouldn't work with everybody. Only 30 percent of trauma sufferers will react in this way.

At the same time, if you want to strengthen the left brain, confronting people with questions that they cannot answer has been found by researchers at the Universities of Santa Barbara and British Columbia to enhance the cognitive mechanisms of the left brain, which oversee learning.

So if you apply trauma in the right way, what you are actually doing is reengineering the brain. Taken as a whole, the totality of the experience—the UFOs, the crop formations, and all the other mysteries—gives rise to truly agonizing questions, and does so in the most vividly surreal context it is possible to imagine.

In other words, one thing our visitors are doing is creating situations that are designed to increase our left-brain functioning. They are trying to improve our ability to think logically.

But for those of us who have the correct response to trauma, it doesn't end there. We are also being given shocks that induce PTSD, thus causing an increase in right-brain function as well.

So there is actually a logic to the whole cockeyed business, and behind it can perhaps be seen an aim: whatever is doing it is trying to improve our mental function. This means that no matter how exploitative it may seem, one of its motives must be to speed up the evolution of the human brain.

If this is the case, then it cannot be that it seeks to exploit us, or not only that, because to increase our brain function is to lead us toward a kind of freedom that we do not now possess. The farmer does not want to teach his steers how to run the slaughterhouse. He wants them only to go peacefully to their deaths.

Nobody who is trying to improve our brain function is interested in our death. But as I discussed earlier in this book, it also seems clear that their interest is in helping us without revealing themselves too early, lest we lose our independence by focusing on them and becoming dependent on them.

That's exactly what would happen if they suddenly appeared now. We'd want the gadgets, and all the pressure of the question would evaporate, and with it their hope of actually rewiring the human brain. Because that's exactly what is seen to happen when exposures such as the ones described in this book take place. The brain changes.

A new world, then. A new mankind beckons, one might think, free and independent, no longer living this strange, veiled life that we know now, but rather made whole, the physical and radiant elements of the species working together toward an increase at present unknown.

When I first walked out into the night woods in early 1986, just getting off my porch was practically impossible. It was like going up a gallows must be.

The fear was actually greater, I think, than the fear of death. It was as if a danger worse than death awaited me out there in the night.

It was not some malodorous demon, though. I came to understand my fear. When I was near the visitors, I saw the world differently. I saw myself as a body moving through experience that was to a degree ordained.

One close-encounter witness wrote that while with them he had seen his whole future life flash past, and now lived in a permanent state of déjà vu. I could well understand his plight. Often, after being with them, I would find that my sense of surprise about life had gone. It was an odd, contradictory feeling, like being trapped and set free at the same time. Everything felt like a coincidence, and nothing was surprising.

This could leave me depressed for days. It felt as if my future, in being revealed to me, had also been leached of meaning.

I could take only a little of this. Almost the moment it started happening, I would turn away. The menace of it was incredible. I would
be in the woods meditating, and suddenly would see some image—
usually a simple thing, like speaking to the grocer, washing my car—
and know with absolute certainty that it *would happen*. Then would
come a creeping terror that I did not understand, and I would leap up
and run for the house and decide, yet again, that I would never, ever
be such a fool as to go out in those woods.

But then I would ask myself, *Why was that so frightening?*

I think that this is because we use life to affect the soul, and if the
future is known, then the energy of spontaneity is lost, and with it our
whole reason for being.

Who we are has become to me the greatest of all mysteries. Who
and what. We present an appearance to ourselves of being a physical
species that has evolved over aeons, reaching intelligence about a hundred thousand years ago, and becoming self-conscious when we began
to make art about forty thousand years ago.

I do not think that this is what we are. It's an illusion that we have
chosen for ourselves. Human bodies are devices that we use to penetrate our attention deeply into the sensory world. But they are not
us. We are something else, come here to rest ourselves and recover
ourselves outside of the endlessness that is our true home, and, above
all, to evolve into something new.

I know what we seek. Back when I was going out in the woods,
among the very few words that my visitors said to me in plain English
were "Have joy." But how do you find it? You find it by dropping the
load of life, and with it arrogance and self-will, something that is far
easier said than done, from my own experience.

We are here to live past our egos, but if we know our future, our
lives will not shock us enough to be effective, or so it would seem.

I suspect that this is the great difference between us and aliens who might be here, and there are likely some mixed into this bubbling stew of being, I would think. I think that they have been here a long time. They are probably the fairy-folk of old, and the silkies and the sylphs, and the distant gods who once roared their civilizing instructions but have since fallen silent.

The gulf between us arises from the fact that their souls and body forms are not divided like ours. Their consciousness extends across the entire spectrum of being, with the result that bodies have an entirely different meaning for them than they do for us.

We feel that our bodies *are* us. My name is Whitley Strieber because that is what I was given at birth. But I was somebody before I had that name. I am still that person. All of us, underneath our names, are somebody more authentic. Personality is a device that is apparently designed to guide us into the sorts of life experiences that we need to have in order to further whatever mysterious quest we are on.

The stakes are very high indeed. They are as high as stakes can get. Unless we can find ourselves before earth ceases to be able to support human bodies in numbers, we are going to find our journey very rudely interrupted.

We are part of the larger body of earth, born out of her, and if she fails, then I would think that we have no recourse. Unless we can enter earthly bodies, we can't enter any bodies at all. It is my impression that much of the sexual manipulation our visitors have engaged in has been about creating bodies not that would enable them to live here but rather that would enable us to continue our quest elsewhere, if we lose earth.

For example, the man who stayed in our woods when we were under threat from the local people, and who followed us to Texas to be sure that we were safe there, was not a normal human being. At times, I could communicate with him the way I did with the others, in the mind. But it was different. His mind was a desperate nest of rage and tension. He could hear thoughts, and at one point we were able to briefly share his experience, which was among the most appalling things that has ever happened to me.

At the moment that it happened, I did not fully understand. What I did know was that I could suddenly hear a great number of voices, and they were all roaring and snarling and wailing, partly in words, partly in feelings, and they were primitive in the extreme. They were savage but they were also in a strange way wonderful. I could hear the striving, the urgency, the longing. Like prisoners clamoring in their cages, or tigers pacing in the zoo.

But these were people, not animals. This was the way our minds sound to our visitors and to this poor man who had been fashioned partly out of them and partly out of us.

I had feared him and disliked him. I had found his constant smoking loathsome and very confusing. Why was he doing this?

He was doing it because he was living an agony of a life, steeped in our savage roar.

I have wanted to hold him, to bring him some kind of comfort, but he's gone from my life now, off down the street in anger and disappointment. When I meditate now, one thing I do is try to make a silence inside myself that can be a sort of refuge for people like him, and he is far from being the only one, I can assure you.

I also know some things about the dead. For years, I meditated with a dead man who had come into reconciliation with himself. He was radiant, and what he was radiating was insight, and with it, joy.

I have seen the joy of the dead, but I have also seen their suffering. I think that they must not possess the filters afforded by the brain, the intricate bridgework that mediates consciousness in such a way that we need not feel the true consequences of our lives.

The dead are not like that. The dead feel it all. I've had a life review and so has my wife. We're both living between the worlds, and we're certainly not alone. Because medicine now brings so many people back from the dead, there are more people in this state now, as I suggested earlier, than ever before.

I have felt the fantastically powerful emotions associated with what is called sin. The regret, the loathing, the blinding horror—I have felt these things while still alive, and I have understood to my core the Master of the Key's immensely potent definition of sin: "denial of the right to thrive."

The way I was before, I would slide past the things that I had done that were hurtful to others. I floated on a cloud of self-justification, something that I am not alone in doing. My inner life was congratulatory. Of course, I worried about the consequences of a book like *Communion* in the lives of others, but I knew that I had been as honest and as accurate as I was able. Still, I pushed away the prospect that I might have been entirely wrong and misled millions of people, spreading not release from lies but just more lies. Had I known what I know now, I would never have allowed it to be published with a cover that telegraphed the idea that it was about alien contact. My life is not about alien contact. It is about contact with a greater humanity.

Being confined as we are in the time stream is an incredibly valuable asset. It really is the pearl of great price. Change of soul is the most valuable gift that life offers, because it is permanent and it takes us another step closer to the freedom that we seek.

But we are in a conundrum. Our planet is running out of time. We're too big. She cannot bear us much longer. As I write this, it is 103°F in Santa Monica, California. Elsewhere in Los Angeles, it is 113°F. All-time record heat. Not only that, the Northwest Passage is open for only the second time since records have been kept. A seagoing yacht, the *Octopus*, has just completed the legendary passage from Atlantic to Pacific across the top of the world, through open water.

Russia has this summer experienced a heat wave of millennial intensity. All over the world, climactic disruptions are causing interruptions to crop formation and ravaging harvests. Where it isn't far too cold, it's far too hot. Where there is not drought, there are catastrophic floods.

And there are so many of us on this planet that if anything goes seriously wrong, an unimaginable catastrophe is going to unfold.

I don't know the future. But I do know that the Master of the Key warned me in 1998 that this was going to happen.

We don't have long. Like it or not, no matter what the deniers say and how hard they pretend, the human species is going down the pro-verbial birth canal. Right on schedule, it seems, as the Age of Aquarius is dawning, mother earth is spilling her waters.

Mankind is going to die, one way or another, to the world that we know now. But, at the same time, mankind is going to be born— literally born again.

I have seen a human being in radiance. He meditated with me for years. He was and is entirely real. He was different from us in one enormous respect that bypasses all concerns about the veil between the living and the dead, and leaps beyond the fear of seeing too much to change: he was in control of his state. He could be physical. I saw him. I touched him. I smelled his skin and felt his hand in mine. Like our visitors, and like all species that have ascended into the state where we are heading, he could control his own wave function. He could transform his entire body from a physical presence into an indeter-minate state, then, while that happens in nature, collapse the wave again into the physical, at will. He could let himself be himself, and by directing his attention to the joy that was in him and was him, express his radiance. I saw this and felt it. It was entirely real, all of it. I am not describing a theoretical being or some sort of an idea. I am describing a man I knew for years.

So also, the Master of the Key was real. I would speculate that he, also, was like the man I meditated with at my cabin, a human being in a state in which the individual can control the degree to which he is a physical entity. It is the next state of man, which, in the fullness of time, nature will bring to all of us who are able to accept it.

From time immemorial, we have lived with the mystery of death. Neanderthal graves have been found in which the deceased has been honored with flowers and decorations of red ocher. Even then, the mystery was with us.

Mankind is evolving. This book is about the direction we will take, and what it will be like in the future, when the veil lifts, and the living and what we call the dead cease to be divided, and the human mind begins to live and function at once inside the stream of time, and above it.

Whether or not we will cling to our familiar material world too long remains to be seen. But in whatever case, earth is going to give up her infant to the greater cosmos.

Although my mind keeps the question of what will happen to us open, my heart trusts that ours will be a living birth. If so, then we will join our voices at last to the timeless chorus of conscious species who, in uncountable ways, are journeying with the universe toward its destiny, and at the same time toward an ecstasy that has no end.

As I come into the last decades of my life, I have tried to communicate in as truthful a manner as possible the remarkable things I have learned and experienced. I have been in far distances, farther than I can ever say, and have seen one clear thing: man is a greater triumph of nature than we know or dare to believe.

One day and surprisingly soon, we will find the wings of understanding, and take flight.

CHAPTER 16
What Is to Come

E VERY FEW MONTHS, SOMEBODY ANNOUNCES that aliens are about to land. This has been going on for more than fifty years, and for all of that time, the announcements have been wrong. In addition, people have been agitating for the U.S. government to disclose its secrets. This, also, has been going on for half a century. In a 1960 letter to Congress, retired CIA director Admiral Roscoe Hillenkoetter wrote, "Behind the scenes, high-ranking Air Force officers are soberly concerned about UFOs. But through official secrecy and ridicule, many citizens are led to believe the unknown flying objects are nonsense." Nothing came of the letter or any of the other efforts at disclosure that took place in that era. Instead, in 1968, the Air Force completed Project Blue Book, which led to its public departure from UFO concerns. Jimmy Carter promised to reveal all, but now won't discuss the matter. When John Podesta was Bill Clinton's chief of staff, he explored the matter. He still advocates disclosure, but the Obama administration shows the same reticence that has been present from the beginning.

Judging from what would transpire if the U.S. government did disclose, it is difficult to believe that this will ever happen. It is less clear that our visitors will hide forever.

I have discussed a number of reasons why they wish to remain concealed, among them the fact that they are doing things to us that, if we understood them, we might wish to resist. It also may be that I am correct about Dr. Von Neumann's concern, and that they cannot fully invest in our reality until we accept them, but somehow this does not ring very true for me. I can see how an untestable concern like that, coming from a top scientist, would be another nail in the coffin of disclosure, but I doubt that it is an actual problem for our visitors.

I also don't think that they are involved with us only at the physical level. This is only the part that we can see, because we are blind to the most important point of contact, which is on the level of conscious energy on the soul. I think that this is also the primary level on which they are real. For them, the physical world that seems to us to be completely central to everything is probably secondary.

It isn't clear to me, as well, that there is anything approaching a consistent policy among our visitors. Only one thing is universal: secrecy. But can the same individuals who are responsible for the crop formations also be responsible for the sheep mutilations taking place a few miles away? On the one hand, a playful, aesthetically conscious, and brilliant presence plays esoteric mathematical and geometric games in fields that are connected in some way to sacred sites of the past. Meanwhile, a short distance away, the blood of animals is removed, their eyes are cored out, their tongues and lips and sexual organs excised, and other mutilations take place.

It is difficult to imagine the same entities doing both things.

Or is it? You can get in a car in Fort Worth and travel in a few minutes from one of the finest art museums in the United States to one of the biggest slaughterhouses. In the Congo, it is possible to find some children receiving education by excellent teachers, while others, perhaps even their siblings, are being forced to fight savage battles as child soldiers.

In fact, the range of human behavior is extremely broad, and we can expect the range of our visitors' activities to be at least as varied, especially given that their perspective on the physical world may be profoundly different from our own.

What might it be like if our visitors were no longer secretive about their actions, and entered the general knowledge of mankind? How might they accomplish this, and why might they do it?

There would no doubt be intense worldwide excitement at first. What are they like? How does their technology work? What are they going to give us?

The world of religion would be the first to be set afire. Universally, religion has approached the conundrum of being by replacing the basic questions of who we are and how we came to be with various sets of beliefs that suggest the presence of higher powers. But what role do our visitors play in these constructs? To the Muslims of Sulawesi, they are djinn. But who might they be to the Christians? Demons, perhaps? Fundamentalist Christians might assume that, as they travel in conveyances, they could not be angels, and are therefore demons. The Catholic Church has taken a different approach. Pope John Paul said that Christians should consider aliens as having human rights. Papal astronomer Guy Consolmagno said in 2010 that he would baptize an alien if asked. In 2005, Brother Consolmagno published a booklet titled *Intelligent Life in the Universe? Catholic Belief and the Search for Extraterrestrial Intelligent Life*, in which he says, "However you picture the universe being created, says Genesis, the essential point is that ultimately it was a deliberate, loving act of a God who exists outside of space and time."

Recent discoveries as outlined by Stephen Hawking in his book

The Grand Design suggest that the big bang didn't need a creator, but that the universe could have emerged out of nothing, without any creative motivator behind it.

It is perfectly possible that aliens would see things Dr. Hawking's way rather than Brother Consolmagno's, in which case the whole human religious enterprise would experience a severe challenge. As matters stand, the rise of fundamentalisms worldwide is a sign of a decline in religious belief, not an increase. As more and more people begin to live by secular assumptions, the believers begin to shrill like cicadas in the autumn, crying more and more loudly against the cold that will inevitably envelop them.

However, religion might not be entirely wrong. There is the possibility, as I have discussed, that conscious life extends into an energetic level that is completely detached from the physical, and that our visitors do not share the barrier between physical and energetic consciousness that so profoundly colors human life and human culture.

If so, one of the first things that we may learn from them is that while god does not exist, the soul does. How the truth about life might then disclose itself to us is at present unclear, except in the respect that it will be the most profound and deeply shocking cultural change that we have ever known.

As I have pointed out in previous chapters, there is something about the close-encounter experience, taken as a whole, that suggests that open contact will hardly be the sweet meeting that at first the whole world will envision. But at first, there will be a completely unprecedented outburst of excitement and euphoria. People will be dancing in the streets. Every religion will be galvanized. Science will be astounded and overawed. Corporations, individuals, governments— everybody will be seeking meetings. Lunatics will be proclaiming their allegiances and connections to the aliens. World leaders will speak in hopeful terms.

But then again, during the spring of 1941, the Ukrainians welcomed the arrival of the Wehrmacht with excited celebration. The German soldiers were seen as liberators and representatives of Western civilization. But then Reichskommisar Erich Koch arrived to establish a government in accordance with Nazi principles, and they found themselves enslaved.

I cannot say that this will happen to us, but I do think that, based on the many bizarre and horrifying stories that have emerged out of the close-encounter experience, euphoria might be an inappropriate reaction to the sudden arrival of large numbers of visitors in open contact with us, especially if they are something very different from what they seem. Even open contact might not relieve the ambiguities associated with them. If there are actually such things as physically real parallel universes, and they are from such a place, then, no matter how hard we try to identify what they are, ambiguities will always continue to prevent us from coming to any final conclusion. Even time might not, under such circumstances, reveal the truth, if only because the true scale of such a reality will be so much larger than we can conceive, especially if alternate histories are a description of actual events, and our visitors are, therefore, no matter how bizarre in appearance, essentially us.

As I have said before, in my own life when I challenged the visitors by setting off in the dark of night to meet them, they responded by elevating me from the status of lab animal to that of student, and proceeded to take me on what I can safely characterize as one of the more interesting courses of study ever advanced to any student.

They have also been helpful to a scientist whom I know well, and I have heard of a number of others who have received support from them. But what of the thousands or perhaps even millions of people who have been abducted and left with no clear idea of what happened to them, except that they were simply kidnapped, subjected to arcane invasions of various sorts, then returned to their homes without the slightest care being taken to explain anything to them? And what of those who did not return?

Within a decade of the arrival of the Spaniards in Mexico, the indigenous culture was completely destroyed, and with it 90 percent of the local population. It was not just Aztec culture that was destroyed but a whole intricate system of cultures entwined across all of Mexico. And they were not simply human-sacrificing savages, not by any means. As Dr. Miguel León-Portilla points out in his book *Aztec Thought and Culture*, civilization had existed in Mexico for two millennia before the arrival of the Spaniards in 1519. After the conquest, Nahuatl scholars produced a treasury of documents in their native language, but using the Latin alphabet, which reveal a highly sophisticated philosophical culture, in many ways more so than what the Spaniards imposed on it. Among other things, there is a richly suggestive body of material about death and the afterlife, much more nuanced than the Catholic beliefs that replaced it.

But this has all been swept away. And will our own culture, also, be swept away on a tide that is more technologically sophisticated but less culturally nuanced? Superior technology stupefied the Aztecs, not superior culture. Of course they engaged in human sacrifice, but so did the Spaniards, in the autos-da-fé of the Inquisition, where the stench of burning hair and flesh was said to smell "sweet" to the Virgin Mary and her baby son.

I confess that I fear very much that human culture will take a terrific beating from contact. Our older cultures, especially, will be vulnerable to being plunged into irrelevance, and one can only hope that Kuiper and Morris were right, and our visitors are restrained by a concern for the deleterious effect that their emergence would have on the developing and evolving richness of human culture and the human soul.

But I also think that very gradually, more clearly focused general contact is getting closer, and I suspect that sooner or later, it will come.

As we move inevitably toward a more unstable environmental situation, our desperation is going to increase more and more. Again and again, as I have been pointing out for years, our visitors have communicated warnings about the peril we are in. And yet these warnings have not been communicated to our leadership, or to the wealthy potentates who spread propaganda that nothing is wrong. Instead, ordinary people, with little access to the powerful, have been chosen to receive the message. So while it has been delivered, it has not reached the right ears.

The best I have been able to do in response to the warnings is to publish *Superstorm*, and see it transformed into a popular film, *The Day After Tomorrow*. But the concept that climate could change with extreme suddenness was dismissed during the period that the film was receiving public notice. Only afterward, when public notice had died away and with it the potential for public pressure, did it emerge that extremely sudden climate change is indeed a possibility.

With both the corporate infrastructure and the third world refusing to take adequate steps to forestall climate change, it seems that it is inevitable. The blazing summers and freezing winters we experience now are a worrisome sign that climate is beginning to oscillate out of control.

If methane begins to outgas from methane hydrates now frozen in the Arctic Ocean, the gas will flood our atmosphere and cause catastrophic short-term warming. This has happened before in geologic history, and has always been accompanied by violent climactic upheavals. As matters stand, methane outgassing from tundra melt has increased 30 percent in recent years, and arctic waters are warmer than ever, so it cannot be long before this happens.

So with mankind apparently sitting in all innocence under this sword of Damocles, why don't our visitors openly warn us now? Why wait?

For all I know, they could show up tomorrow, warning in hand. Unfortunately, though, if it isn't backed up by robust technological support of some kind, at this point we are going to experience extreme climate change no matter if we stopped all emissions tomorrow.

Still, though, for most of us, whether or not climate change will come is an open question. If our visitors are waiting to save us until the last minute, it has already passed. So they aren't waiting for the last minute. Therefore, if this is relevant to their thinking at all, they must be waiting until we are desperate—unless, of course, they have no intention of interrupting the process of dieback that is likely to unfold.

It's certainly possible that they would not want us to be able to leave earth in numbers, and also that their open emergence will lead to our scientific establishment finally studying their technology seriously enough to actually understand it.

In any case, their failure to reveal themselves now does suggest that they are not here to rescue us but for some other reason or, more probably, for many other reasons.

A single human being might save a kitten, cut off the head of a chicken, pray, fornicate, slap a spouse, and embrace the same spouse, all in an hour. So perhaps it isn't so improbable that the same complex intelligence that we are facing would act in many different ways, some of them tremendously challenging to us. If contact meant that what is apparently happening on Sulawesi and in Brazil would extend to the entire world, or abductions and implantations would become a general human experience, then the danger is incredible. But if it means that millions of people will end up in a school such as the one I have attended, then a case can be made for embracing it. In reality, though, it is going to mean a complex mix of different interactions and experiences, characterized by a great deal of panic, confusion, and misinformation. I was raped, my sexual materials taken from me, subsequently shown a baby, and left to live in a permanent state of stress but also shown new ways of thinking, and a hidden level of being that is sublime.

The knowledge I have gained is of incalculable value to me—which it had better be, because I have paid a high price for it, and I am not alone. This same pattern repeats in one way or another in the lives of most people who have extensive contact.

As the United States is unlikely to admit that it knows that the visitors are real, if would seem that unless something completely unforeseen happens (always, perhaps, the leading possibility), then they are not going to initiate contact, if at all, unless they must.

The question, of course, is who and where? In the 1950s, it certainly appeared that the United States would be the target. Nothing happened. In the 1980s, Brazil was the center of UFO activity in the world. There was no formal contact. In the 1990s, it was Mexico. Once again, the phenomenon built up to a climax of sightings, then subsided. As this is being written, the focus of UFO activity is China. If the reports are truthful (always an issue when UFOs are mixed with the Internet), then eight Chinese airports had to be closed down in the first nine months of 2010 because of UFO close approaches. As yet, though, there has been no moment when demonstrably nonhuman entities have interacted in a public context with human beings.

It is important to assume nothing; to study what is accessible to study, which is the physical evidence; and to methodically close the outstanding questions as we become able to do so.

We can determine the operational characteristics of unidentified flying objects. We can identify much about implants and analyze the experiences of those who carry them in their bodies. We can do far more thorough analysis of the crop formations. We can analyze the carcasses of animals destroyed in mutilation attacks. Perhaps in the future we will be able to make some sense of conscious energy.

We have come into being on a tiny speck of a planet lost in a vastness of unimaginable complexity and incredible age that appears to be expanding into an eternal void. This is where we truly are. There is something here among us that acts in an intelligent manner, but not in ways that we might act. Coming to terms with it offers a reasonable chance of opening rich new avenues of knowledge. Continuing to deny its existence is an arid and bankrupt position that offers no gain and the potential for great loss.

We do not know who or what this presence is. But then again, there is another mystery on this little planet of ours that is at least as great: it is the mystery of this ape that has suddenly looked up, and begun to count the stars.

The future of the human species is unimaginable. If I have learned one thing, though, over the lifetime I have spent in the school of our visitors, it is this: they are not the greater mystery. We are the greater mystery, and in coming to terms with the challenges that they represent, we are inevitably going to advance the most potent of all questions: Who are we?

ACKNOWLEDGMENTS

I CANNOT COUNT THE NUMBER OF PEOPLE WHOSE NARRATIVES OF close encounter have illuminated my own thinking about this enigma. Additionally, there is a whole community of researchers, many of them genuinely dedicated to objective and thoughtful analysis, whose work has preceded my own and without whose efforts mine would have been so much less.

I have benefited greatly from the work of Dr. Paul Hill, whose determination and love of the truth led him to write one of the seminal books in the field, *Unconventional Flying Objects*. Dr. Jacques Vallée's *Confrontations* was helpful. I owe thanks also to Bob Pratt for his *UFO Danger Zone*, and to Frank Feschino for his careful struggle to reveal the truth about concealed military responses to this strange presence in such books as *Shoot Them Down!: the Flying Saucer Air Wars of 1952*. Keith Chester's research into the period of the 1930s and 1940s in *Strange Company* was of great value to me, as was Leslie Kean's *UFOs: Generals, Pilots, and Government Officials Go on the Record* and Dr. Kenneth Ring's *The Omega Project: Near-Death Experiences, UFO Encounters and Mind at Large*.

The work of the late Dr. John Mack illuminated and dignified the close-encounter experience, and that of Dr. Roger Leir and the surgeons who work with him has opened the door to the possibility of analyzing the physical evidence involved. I owe the two of them thanks, as well as the late Dr. William Mallow of the Southwest Research Institute, for his willingness to test unusual objects with state-of-the-art equipment and to report his findings objectively.

I must also thank Dr. Jeffrey Kripal for the courage to embrace a dangerous revolutionary like me, and his insight into just how real that danger is, and Mitch Horowitz, my editor at Tarcher/Penguin, who was willing to leap into this minefield despite his knowledge of the perils of doing so.

I cannot begin to thank Anne Strieber for the enormous support she has given me over the twenty-five-year ordeal of the experience that we have shared with complete and frank intimacy. It was her determination to preserve the question, and her insight into the importance of doing so, that has formed the foundation of my own thinking. Her discovery, after reading thousands upon thousands of narratives of close encounter, that it was much more nuanced than a simple matter of "alien contact" was our first great intellectual breakthrough, as she understood the fact that there is an entirely unexpected but profound connection between visions of the dead and close encounters of the third kind. She also brought to the table the additional insight, and the scientific discoveries that support it, that questions that cannot be closed actually affect the brain, driving it to reform itself in response to the challenge.

So this book, and the whole of my work and indeed my entire life, are profoundly dependent upon her intellect and her carefully open mind, for which I am more grateful than it is possible to say.

ABOUT THE AUTHOR

WHITLEY STRIEBER is the internationally bestselling author of more than twenty novels and works of nonfiction, among them the landmark work *Communion,* his account of a close encounter of the third kind that took place in December of 1985. He is also the author of *The Wolfen, The Hunger,* and *The Coming Global Superstorm,* all of which were made into feature films, most recently *Superstorm* as *The Day After Tomorrow.* He lives in California.